Guide to Good Writing

by Diane P. Kostick

illustrated by Susan Kropa

To Andy, Yuri, and Jolie

Special thanks to Miriam Lykke, editor, proofreader, and guardian angel; to True Kong, computer consultant and friend; and to Hubert Fischer, computer teacher, dedicated teacher, and friend.

Product Manager: Mina McMullin
Editors: Kathy Zaun, Jill Kaufman
Cover Design: Signature Design Group, Inc.
Interior Design: Good Neighbor Press

GOOD APPLE
A Division of Frank Schaffer Publications, Inc.
23740 Hawthorne Blvd.
Torrance, CA 90505

ISBN 1-56417-965-6

About This Book

Guide to Good Writing has been designed to help students and others develop the essential writing habits and skills they need to be effective writers. The book leads writers step-by-step through each phase of the writing process and beyond—from brainstorming and drafting techniques to editing, conferencing, publishing, portfolios, and so much more. It features a series of lessons writers can engage in to help them learn how to write more effectively and how to feel good about writing. The goal of *Guide to Good Writing* is to assist teachers in helping their students master the writing process.

Pages 6–10 contain a *Teacher's Guide*. This guide is extremely helpful as it provides wonderful teaching ideas and suggestions of ways to best use certain materials presented in each chapter. Be sure to read the information given about each chapter before you teach it.

Each of the chapters in this book begins with a **graphic organizer**. These graphic organizers highlight the ideas covered in each chapter. They may be photocopied and given to students to put into portfolios for reference, or they may be made into transparencies and used in the classroom on the overhead projector to stimulate student discussions.

Also included in the chapters are **activities** to give students practice in the skills or concepts being featured. These activities are designed to energize teachers and student-writers in all the writing process stages. **Checklists** are also scattered throughout the book and have been included to enable teachers and students to evaluate and monitor students' writing progress. The checklists may also be photocopied and given to students to be placed in their portfolios, or they may be distributed to students for their use at appropriate stages in the writing process. Similar to checklists, students and teachers will also find **writers' tips** and **hotline pages** in this book. They, too, can be used as self-editing guidelines.

A series of **almost-blank pages** can also be found in this book. Students can use these for writing drafts and final copies. You might consider photocopying these pages in different colors for students in order to emphasize the particular phase of the writing process they are working on. This will help students vividly see that writing is a process and that it takes many layers of diligent work in order to be successful writers.

A list of **writing ideas**, a **glossary**, an **index**, and a **bibliography** used to develop *Guide to Good Writing* appear at the back of the book for your convenience.

By following the exercises, tips, ideas, and models in *Guide to Good Writing*, students and teachers will feel more in touch, more at ease, more in control, and better satisfied with their writing and their writing experiences.

WELCOME

Students, teachers, parents, and writers—this book is dedicated to helping you.

TABLE OF CONTENTS

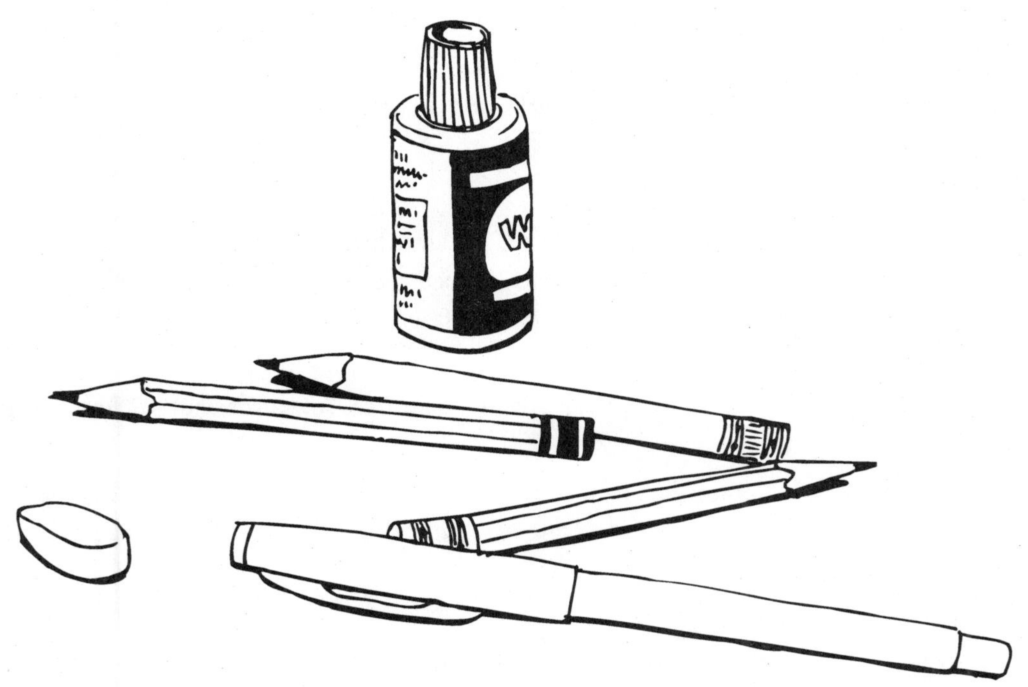

TEACHER'S GUIDE

As most chapters in this book contain student activity pages, this *Teacher's Guide* offers suggestions on how to use these student activity pages. Photocopy these activity pages and distribute them to students. You may also want to photocopy the information presented at the front of each chapter to give to the students.

Chapter 1—The Writing Teacher . . .

p. 14 As a writing teacher, you should engage in all, or as many of the activities listed on page 14 as possible. Refer to this page from time to time to remind yourself of good habits all writing teachers need. Make a copy of page 14 and put it in your portfolio or notebook.

Chapter 2—Get to Know Yourself as a Reader

pp. 16–17 Discuss with students the kinds of books they like to read. You might like to make a list of these books on the board. Distribute copies of the reading surveys on pages 16–17 to students. Have them complete the pages. Discuss students' responses.

pp. 18–20 Distribute copies of these pages to students and ask them to fill in their responses. Discuss students' comments.

Chapter 3—Know Yourself as a Writer

pp. 22–26 Distribute copies of pages 22–26 to students. Ask them to write their responses to the inquiries. Using the results of their responses, hold a class discussion about the topic of writing. Make a list of students' ideas about writing on the board, or write them on tagboard and display their ideas in the classroom.

p. 27 Give students a copy of the "Writing is . . ." brainstorming page. After five minutes of free writing, have them share their ideas.

pp. 28–29 Give students copies of these pages. Have students use their ideas from page 27, "Writing is . . .", to write their ideas of what they think writing is. Have students who are willing to share their ideas present their ideas to the class.

Chapter 4—A Writer's Notebook

pp. 31–32 Give students copies of pages 31–32 and have them discuss the writers' tips on page 32. Have them put these pages in their notebooks or portfolios for later reference.

p. 33 Give students copies of this page at the beginning of each month. Tell students to fill in the month and dates. Have them keep track of when they write and what kind of writing they do. For example: Mon., Jan. 2. *Wrote in my journal for 5 minutes and described my birthday.* Students should keep all their calendar pages in their notebooks or in their portfolios.

p. 34 Students can fill out this page and put it in their portfolios or notebooks to keep track of the kinds of writing they include in them.

Chapter 5—Getting Ready to Write

pp. 36–37 Give students copies of these pages, or go over the information with them.

p. 38 Give students copies of page 38. Ask them to put check marks in all boxes that describe them as writers. Have them keep this page in their portfolios or notebooks and add checks to the boxes when appropriate.

p. 39 Give students copies of the graphic organizer on page 39. After a discussion of the items on this page, have students put this sheet in their portfolios or notebooks to be referred to as necessary.

Chapter 6—The Writer's Workshop

p. 41 This chapter explains the writer's workshop. Carefully read and discuss the information on page 41 about the workshop with the students. The writer's workshop is a writing process which uses an orderly approach to writing going from the first stage of putting words on paper to finally publishing a manuscript. The writer's workshop technique allows you to grow as a writer with the help of fellow writers—teachers and peers. For writers engaged in the workshop, writing is no longer a lonely business; it becomes a community of collaborators interested in improving each other's writing. Writers using a workshop approach learn that it is normal to write and revise, to rewrite and edit, to discuss and change their pieces of writing in order to make each manuscript the best that it can be.

pp. 42–43 Give copies of pages 42–43 to students. Discuss the *Tenets of Writing* with students and then have them put both of these pages in their portfolios or notebooks to be reviewed as needed.

Chapter 7—Audience

pp. 45–46 Discuss pages 45–46 with students. Have students put them in their portfolios or notebooks.

p. 47 Have students use their writing portfolios to complete *Section One—I wrote . . . My audience is . . .* They should put page 47 in their notebooks or portfolios and add to *Section Two—I will write . . . My audience will be . . .* during the course of the year.

p. 48 Have students write letters requesting a sleepover to a parent and to a friend. Discuss the difference in language, or tone and mood, of letters written to their parents and letters written to their friends. Ask them why they think writers change the tone of their writing based on the audience they are addressing.

p. 49 After a class discussion about the kinds of foods offered in the school cafeteria, have students use page 49 to write letters to the principal asking that a larger variety of foods be offered in the cafeteria.

p. 50 Have students look through their portfolios and put a check in the box next to each type of audience for whom they have written in the last month. Have them keep this page in their notebooks or portfolios and add checks to the boxes whenever they write for a new audience.

p. 51 Students can keep this page in their portfolios or notebooks to refer to after they have selected their topic and are ready to focus on writing. This page reminds students of their purpose for writing and will help them establish the tone, mood, and language they use in their work.

Chapter 8—Brainstorming

p. 54 Make an acetate of the four brainstorming samples on page 54. Use the information on the page with students to discuss different brainstorming techniques. Ask students if they think one technique has more "merit" or is easier to use than another, and ask them to state why they think this. Tell students to keep this page in their portfolios or notebooks to refer to as needed.

p. 55 Have students quickly jot down their responses to the word "Yellow" which is in the center of the page. The color word could be changed if "Yellow" does not seem appropriate. Next, hold a discussion on students' responses to the color word. This page could become the basis for a poem, essay, or story with "Yellow" as the topic.

pp. 56–58 Give students a copy of each of these pages to use to brainstorm ideas for writing.

pp. 59–60 Discuss the contents of each of these pages with students and then have them put these pages in their notebooks or portfolios for future reference.

Chapter 9—First Draft

p. 63 Discuss the ideas on this page and then have students place these tips in their notebooks or portfolios so they can refer to them as needed.

pp. 64–65 A good way for you and your students to keep track of each phase of the writing process would be to photocopy each phase on a different color of paper. Give copies of pages 64–65 to students and have them write their first drafts of a piece of writing on these pages. Students should supplement these pages with notebook paper if necessary.

Chapter 10—Self-Editing

p. 68 Discuss each item contained in the *Self-Editing Guidelines* with students and have them put this page in their notebooks or portfolios.

p. 69 This activity is a wonderful way for students to practice editing. Have students look for the 14 errors in this piece of writing and make their corrections in red directly on the page.

p. 70 Make an acetate of the Answer Key for *When Man Met Dog*, page 70. Have students correct their own papers or have them exchange papers with other students. Discuss each error and its correction in the story with students.

pp. 71–73 Have students use these pages to self-edit one of their manuscripts.

Chapter 11—Second Draft

pp. 76–77 Make copies of the *Second Draft Editing Guidelines* for students to use to help each other edit their second drafts.

pp. 78–79 Photocopy pages 78–79 on a different color of paper than you used for pages 64–65. Have students use these pages to write second drafts of their manuscripts. Students should supplement these pages with notebook paper if necessary.

Chapter 12—Peer Editing

pp. 81–84 Make many copies of Peer Editing Forms #1–#4. Have them available for students to use as they edit each other's papers. You could assign students to use one form or another, or you could allow students to use the form they feel most comfortable with.

Chapter 13—Conferencing

p. 87 To complete this page, students will need to take it and their manuscript to a writing conference with you or with their peers. The completion of this page can then become the basis for a discussion of the manuscript and, therefore, the editing of it.

pp. 88–89 These pages should be completed by the writers and by their editors during a writer's conference focused on their pieces of writing.

Chapter 14—Proofreading

pp. 92–93 Give students copies of the *Proofreader's Guidesheet* and *Proofreader's Guidesheet Checklist.* Have them available as students are editing each other's manuscripts. Students can keep them in their notebooks or portfolios when not in use.

Chapter 15—Final Copy

p. 96 Give students a copy of page 96 to put in their notebooks or portfolios when they are not using it to edit a manuscript. It contains a list of rules students can follow to attain a nice final copy of a manuscript.
pp. 97–98 Photocopy pages 97–98 on a different color of paper than you used for pages 64–65 and 78–79. Have students use these pages to write final copies of their manuscripts.

Chapter 16—Sharing

p. 101 Ask students to look through their notebooks or portfolios and write the titles of five manuscripts and the audience for which each was intended. Students should keep this page in their portfolios or notebooks and add to it the titles and audiences of all manuscripts completed in the future.

p. 102 Have students use this page to keep track of the ways in which they have shared their manuscripts during the course of the school year. They should keep it in their portfolios or notebooks.

Chapter 17—Publishing

pp. 105–107 Have students keep these pages in their portfolios or notebooks. Students should put check marks in the boxes to indicate the ways in which they publish their manuscripts over the course of the year.

pp. 108–109 These pages contain the addresses of publishing companies students may want to send their manuscripts to to try to get published. Be sure students keep copies of these pages in their portfolios or notebooks.

pp. 110–112 These pages contain general information and specific rules students should follow if they sincerely want to get published. Copies of these pages should be kept in students' portfolios or notebooks.

Chapter 18—Portfolios

pp. 116–121 At the end of each semester, or just before the end of the school year, give copies of these pages to students. Ask them to look through their portfolios and assess their work using these pages.

pp. 122–123 Have students examine the contents of their portfolios and evaluate the contents by putting a check mark in each box on these pages to indicate the different kinds of writing represented in their portfolios. Take a survey of the kinds of writing students in your class have completed over the course of the school year.

Chapter 19—Word Processing

p. 125 Encourage your students to use word processing whenever possible. It makes the process of writing much easier, and it makes the final product much more readable and visually appealing.

Chapter 20—Student Samples

pp. 127–163 The examples contained in this chapter are by no means perfect. They are of pieces of writing produced by students at Barrington Middle Prairie Campus in Barrington, IL. They are intended to serve as examples of how students at this age level write poetry, narratives, short stories, and expository essays. You could photocopy the samples and use them for class discussion before students begin a piece of writing, or you could discuss the merits of each piece of writing so students can learn what is successful and what is not successful in these student samples. Of course, students will also benefit from modeling their writing after professional writers whose work they have seen in textbooks, novels, journals, newspapers, and magazines.

Eventually, students will move away from the models and their own writing will become models for themselves. The student samples merely provide students with starting points for various kinds of writing.

pp. 129–130 Discuss acrostic poems with students and read the student samples on page 129. Then have students write their own acrostic poems on page 130. Have several students share their Awesome Acrostics with the whole class.

p. 134 Give students copies of page 134 that they can use to write phrase completion poems. When students have written their poems, ask for volunteers to share their poems with the class.

p. 140 After students have had time to write their gender poems, have students volunteer to share their poems with the class.

pp. 143–144 Using page 143, ask students to brainstorm words for each of the four seasons. They can then write a poem with one of the seasons as its focus on page 144. Have students share their poems with the class.

pp. 156–157 Ask students to make a list of people they consider heroes. Write the names of student heroes on the board. After a class discussion of why the heroes were chosen by the students, have students select one name from their list and write a story about their hero. The stories could be fiction or nonfiction.

pp. 160–161 Hold a class discussion on people, places, and events that could be focal points for short stories. Then have students complete their own lists of people, places, and events. They should use their lists to write their own short stories.

Chapter 21—Writing Ideas

pp. 165–170 Students can keep this list of writing ideas in their portfolios or in their notebooks to be used as needed throughout the year. Have students add writing prompts to the list whenever they think of additional writing ideas.

CHAPTER 1
THE WRITING TEACHER...

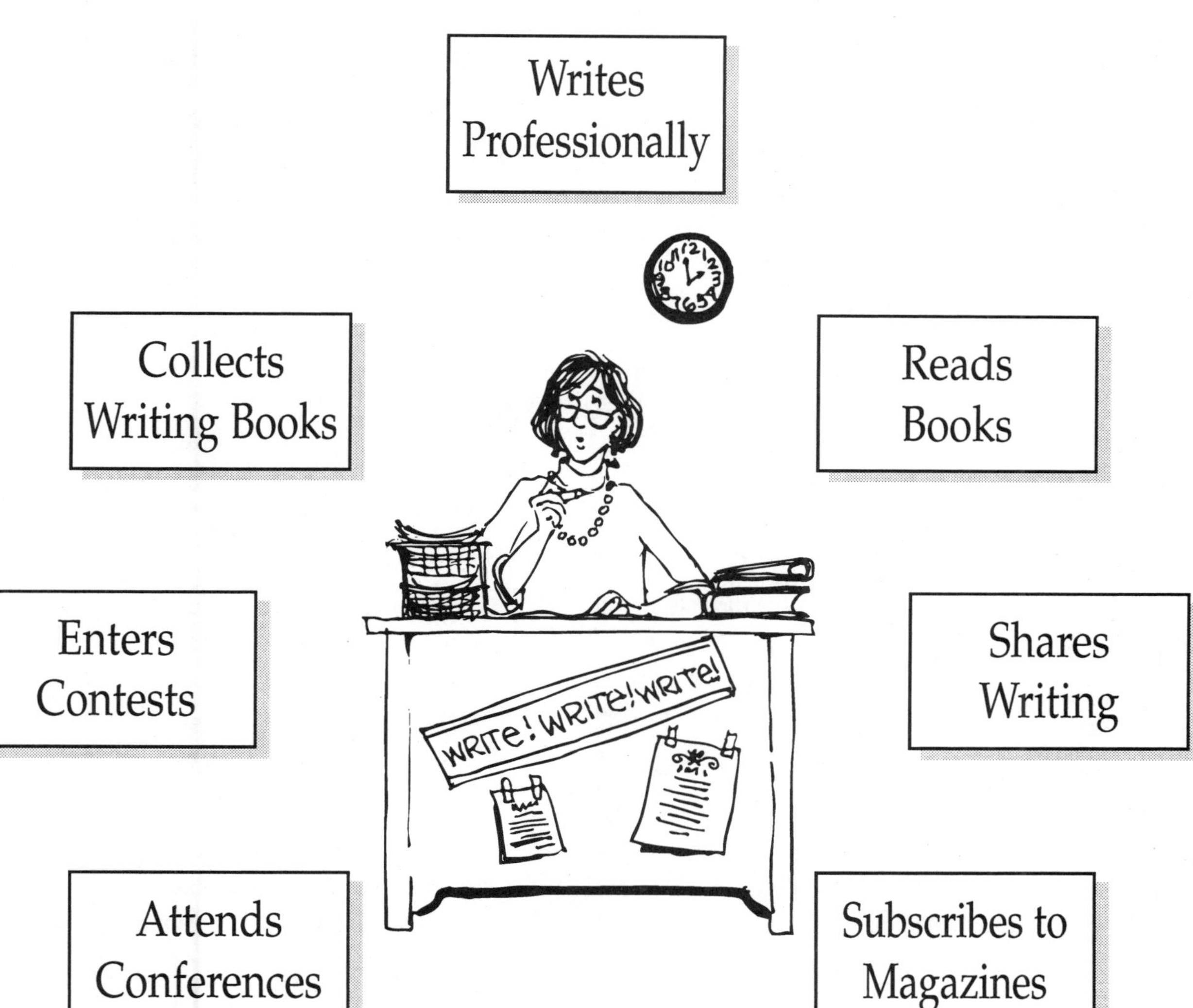

Participates in the Writer's Workshop

THE WRITING TEACHER

Teachers who teach writing should be teachers who write. To be effective, writing teachers must take on the role they ask their students to assume. English or language arts teachers routinely require their students to write book reports, research papers, poems, letters, thank-you notes, and essays. And they often give students specific topics on which to write. However, few teachers ever do the assignments they give their students. For example, how many teachers actually take the time to write a poem, a research paper, or an essay while their students are working on these same projects?

Over the past ten years, whenever I assign my students a writing task, I perform that task, too. If I ask them to read a biography for a book report, I read a biography and also write a book report. Then I share the results of my reading and writing with my students. I do this because I want them to observe me doing what I have asked them to do. It also gives me the chance to experience how easy or how difficult the assignment is. I want my students to know that I understand the effort they are putting forth to complete the assignment I have given them.

When I write with my students, I participate with them in the writing process. I brainstorm, draft, revise, rewrite, edit, polish, and present my writing to them. Using this technique in the classroom enables me to encounter with my students the ups and downs, frustrations and failures, joys and pleasures that I face as a writer. It also says to them, "Writing matters to me." It says to them, "I know what you are going through because I have also experienced it." It says to them, "I'm one with you; we are writers."

In her book *In the Middle,* Nancie Atwell, famed author and teacher, stresses the importance of the teacher as a writer. To teach writing, Atwell believes "we needed to find a way to break with the fine old tradition that had governed our (English teachers) previous curriculum efforts, the one that bore the motto, 'Let's not reinvent the wheel.' To do that, I needed to climb down from my secondary English high horse and find a way to learn with my colleagues just as I was learning with my kids" (how to write, free of usual classroom restrictions).

As Atwell also wanted other teachers to learn about the importance of writing with their students, she developed the Boothbay Summer Writing Project in which she focuses on giving teachers personal writing experiences. In summary, Atwell says of the workshop that first, teachers gave themselves time to write. Next, they gave themselves the authority to write. Finally, they gave themselves diverse personal experiences of writing. The process worked. Participants returned to school in the fall ready to implement what they had learned in the workshop. They were now ready to write with their students which resulted in a complete change in the way in which they taught writing. Writing and sharing the process with their students created a writing community in their classrooms. It freed teachers of the ingrained English teacher pattern in which the teacher assigns a piece of writing; the students write the manuscripts; they turn them in; the teacher corrects the manuscripts; and he or she hands them back to the students with grades and lots of red-pen corrections on them.

The teachers who participated in the Boothbay Summer Writing Project learned that there is a need to take responsibility for improving their own writing, a need to attend writing conferences, a need to read writing magazines, and a need to do what they ask their students to do—write and write and write.

Out of the Boothbay Summer Writing Project came the realization that both teachers and their students must have these things:

- regular chunks of time during which to write,
- their own topics to write about,
- a response to their writing,
- an opportunity to learn writing mechanics in context, and
- a chance to write and share in a nonstressful environment.

> Taking time to write with students
> is essential for all teachers who teach writing.

The Writing Teacher Checklist

Complete the writing teacher survey below by putting a check in the box before each statement that describes you.

Taking time to write with students is essential for all teachers who teach writing. Not to do so sends the wrong message to students. By making a commitment to writing with students, teachers will truly become writing teachers, not just teachers who teach writing. As a writing teacher, you should be doing all, or as many of the activities below as possible.

As a writing teacher, I . . .

- ☐ encourage my students to get published.
- ☐ read professional magazines.
- ☐ read books I know my students are reading.
- ☐ attend professional conferences.
- ☐ read writing magazines.
- ☐ write notes to my students and their parents.
- ☐ attend writers' workshops.
- ☐ enter writing contests.
- ☐ write with my students.
- ☐ let my students see me writing.
- ☐ share my writing with my students.
- ☐ have a collection of books about writing.
- ☐ write, write, write.

Name ______________________ Date__________

6. How do you go about choosing books to read? ______________________

7. Who is your favorite author? ______________________

8. What do you like about his or her books? ______________________

9. What qualities do you look for when selecting a book to read? ______________________

10. Make a list of the books you have read in the last year. ______________________

Name ______________________________ Date______________

Know Yourself as a Reader

Book Survey

Complete the survey below and on pages 19–20 to know yourself as a reader. Share your reactions with your teacher and your classmates.

1. What book are you currently reading? ______________________________

____

2. Who is the author? ______________________________

3. Do you think the title is appropriate? Why or why not? ______________________________

____

____

____

4. What is the setting of the story? How is it important to the book? ______________________________

____

____

____

5. Who is the main character, or protagonist, in the book? ______________________________

How do you know this person is the protagonist? ______________________________

____

____

____

6. How does the protagonist make you feel and why? ______________________________

____

____

____

____

Name ______________________________ Date______________

7. To date, how does this story make you feel? ______________________________

8. At this time as you read the book, what do you think the author's point or message is?

9. What problem does the protagonist face? ______________________________

10. Does the story seem real? ____________ Why or why not? ______________

11. Write a review of this book which you would be willing to share with a peer, your teacher, or your classmates. Give a brief description of the protagonist or another character in the story who interests you.

12. What does the author do to get you to like or dislike this book? ______________

Name ______________________________ Date__________

13. Write your mom or dad, another student in this class, or your teacher a letter about the book. Give detailed information about the book's characters, plot, setting, mood, and theme.

Dear ____________________,

CHAPTER 3

KNOW YOURSELF AS A WRITER

Name ______________________ Date______________

Know Yourself as a Writer

"If you want to write—if you are bursting with things that need putting down on paper—remember that the story of how you became a writer has already begun."
—Phyllis Reynolds Naylor

Complete the writer's survey below and on pages 23–26 to know yourself as a writer. Be as specific as you can when you respond to each question. You may need to complete this survey over a period of time, rather than at one writing period.

1. What do you have to do in order to become a good writer? ______________________

2. What is the easiest part of writing for you?______________________

3. What do you write well? Why? ______________________

Name ______________________________ Date__________

4. What is the hardest part of writing for you? ____________________

5. What do you need to work on? ____________________

6. How do you come up with ideas for writing? ____________________

7. What do you feel are the qualities of good writing? ____________________

Name ______________________________ Date______________

8. What type of writing do you do? Why? ______________________________

9. What is the best piece of writing you have ever done? What makes it good? ______________

10. Why is it important to be able to write well? ______________________________

Name ______________________________ Date__________

11. What do you like about writing? ______________________________

12. How did you learn to write? ______________________________

13. Do you keep samples of your writing from year to year? Why or why not? ______________

Name ______________________________ Date__________

14. Who are your favorite writers? Why?

15. List three areas that are of interest to you and which could serve as topics for writing.

16. What is the most interesting piece of writing you have ever read? Why did you like it?

Name ______________________________ Date ______________

Writing is . . . (continued)

CHAPTER 4

A WRITER'S NOTEBOOK

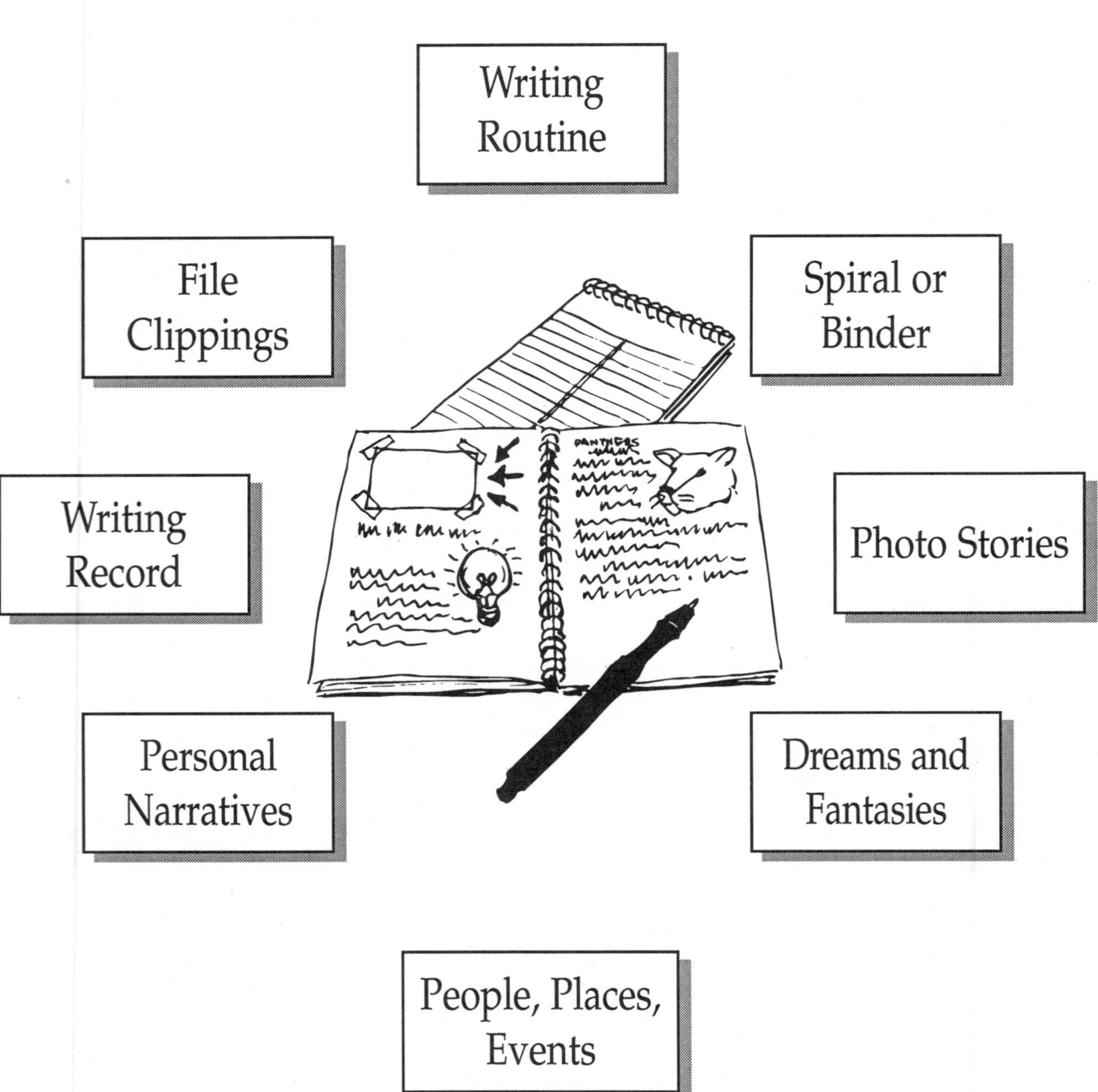

A WRITER'S NOTEBOOK

"Think, too, about your notebook. It is important.
This is your equipment, like hammer and nails to a carpenter."
—Natalie Goldberg

Most writers keep notebooks. The size, shape, and kind of notebooks they keep are as individual as writers. Some writers like yellow-paper legal pads; some prefer spiral notebooks; while others use three-ring binders and loose-leaf paper. The kind of notebook isn't important. What is important is what writers keep in their notebooks. Some writers have two notebooks—one for their writings, and one for writings they admire or find interesting or funny. Some writers clip and tape favorite articles, cartoons, advice columns, sports data, obituaries, speeches, jokes, riddles, research information, and many other kinds of writing in their notebooks. Some use their notebooks to record their own life experiences, goals and aspirations, victories and defeats, dreams and nightmares.

Maybe you'll decide to get two notebooks. A small one that might slip into your pocket is nice because you can take it wherever you go and be ready to jot down your reactions to whatever you see, hear, feel, taste, or touch. You can also keep a bigger one in which to paste, tape, or glue stories and articles that interest you.

Once you have chosen your notebooks, get into the habit of using them. After all, writers write. When you have your notebooks, you will have the means to keep track of your writing as well as a place to store ideas for future pieces you want to write. On page 32 is a list telling you what writers use notebooks for. Keep this handy in your portfolio, notebook, or other safe place to refer to when necessary.

Writers' Tips—Writer's Notebook

Below is a list telling you what writers use notebooks for. Keep this handy in your portfolio, notebook, or other safe place to refer to when necessary.

A writer's notebook is used to . . .

- record announcements and minutes for a club you belong to.
- list what you want for your birthday.
- write directions to a friend's house.
- keep track of secret wishes, dreams, and fantasies.
- figure out your problems.
- express anger with someone in a constructive way.
- write your opinion when you don't want others to see it.
- expand your vocabulary.
- write what's in your head.
- copy something that you have enjoyed reading.
- hold your thoughts, observations, and bits of wit and wisdom.
- jot down conversations you overhear which can be used later to create realistic dialogues for a piece of writing you are doing.
- help you get a sense of being a "professional" writer.
- help you grow as a writer.

Name ______________________________ Date__________

A Writer's Notebook Calendar

Cut out and paste the calendar below inside your writer's notebook. Write the month on the line and the dates in the boxes. Use the calendar to keep track of when you write and what you write. Over time, the calendar will show you what kind of writing habits you have. With this information, you will know when and what you prefer to write. You will be able to establish a schedule of writing which is what all writers do.

Month ______________________ **My Writer's Notebook Calendar**

Sunday	Monday	Tuesday	Wednesday	Thursday	Friday	Saturday

Name ______________________________ Date______________

A Writer's Notebook Checklist

Below is a list of different kinds of writing you might like to include in your writer's notebook. Put a check mark (✓) next to each item on the list after you have entered an example of it in your notebook.

- ☐ fairy tales
- ☐ myths
- ☐ fables
- ☐ ballads
- ☐ haiku poems
- ☐ thank-you notes
- ☐ fantasies
- ☐ concrete poems
- ☐ comparisons
- ☐ questions
- ☐ letters
- ☐ science fiction pieces
- ☐ plays
- ☐ scripts
- ☐ lists
- ☐ interviews
- ☐ sports stories
- ☐ announcements
- ☐ folktales
- ☐ legends
- ☐ how-tos
- ☐ acrostics
- ☐ free verse
- ☐ limericks
- ☐ future thinking pieces
- ☐ cinquains
- ☐ persuasive pieces
- ☐ crossword puzzles
- ☐ stories
- ☐ songs
- ☐ contest entries
- ☐ mysteries
- ☐ ads
- ☐ quotations

Chapter 5

Getting Ready to Write

Gather Tools

Find a Spot to Write

Know Your Audience

Set Goals

Think of Ideas

Write by Making Lists

Write at Your Best Time

Write About Your Life Experiences

GETTING READY TO WRITE

"The trouble with writing starts right at the beginning. There you sit, pencil in hand, a blank sheet of paper before you, and you don't know how to start."

—Rudolf Flesch

When you are given a writing assignment, do you ever think ". . . but I don't have anything to write about"? This may be an honest reaction, but if you think for just a moment, you will realize that you have many ideas you can write about. Everyone has had myriads of life experiences—all of which provide a solid basis for many interesting writing topics.

To get started, think about a special friend or even a pet. Or, remember a special birthday party or family reunion. Perhaps you have been a victim of some injustice—large or small—at one time or another. All of these life experience topics are perfect for creating stories, poems, plays, essays, character sketches, mysteries, westerns, or high-adventure stories.

A good way to decide what to write about is to make yourself aware of all of your potential writing topics. To begin, make a list of story starters based on your personal experiences. Your list might begin like this:

- Things I like to do . . .
- Chores I hate . . .
- The best movie I have ever seen . . .
- My favorite food . . .
- If I could travel anywhere, it would be to . . .
- Three things that make me angry are . . .
- Awards I have received . . .
- I was proudest when . . .
- I feel responsible when . . .
- The happiest day of my life was . . .

With your list of personal likes and dislikes, pleasures and pains, you are ready to begin the writing process. As you begin to have confidence in your writing, keep in mind that your writing is valuable to others as well as to you. For example, have you ever wondered why your mother keeps the Mother's Day poem you wrote in school for her when you were seven, or why your grandfather uses the postcard you sent him from summer camp as his favorite bookmark? Both of these pieces of writing are treasured because the receivers know that these pieces symbolize the fact that you took time to put your thoughts, ideas, and expressions of love on paper to be shared with them.

Name ______________________________ Date______________

Getting Ready to Write

Put a check mark (✓) next to each item that describes you as a writer. Then put this sheet in your portfolio or writer's notebook and refer to it as needed. Continue to put check marks as you expand your habits as a writer.

As a writer, I . . .

- ☐ have a writing routine and establish writing goals.
- ☐ write about my ideas, thoughts, and feelings.
- ☐ observe the world around me and record my observations.
- ☐ use my life experiences as content of poems, stories, letters, etc.
- ☐ collect ads, photos, newspaper clippings, dialogues.
- ☐ doodle, sketch, or create cartoons.
- ☐ read magazines, books, cartoons, "how-to" books, mysteries, classics, romance novels, biographies, autobiographies, and more.
- ☐ write often.
- ☐ look for and enjoy facts and details.
- ☐ write about what I like or dislike, what makes me happy or sad, etc.
- ☐ keep journals and files full of writing ideas.
- ☐ look for fresh ideas all the time.
- ☐ write, write, write.

THE WRITER'S WORKSHOP

"Sometimes you want to write something, make it really good, polish it, and then share it with others. To do this, focus on the process of writing."

—from World of Language (Silver Burdett & Ginn)

The writer's workshop is a series of six steps—prewriting, drafting, simmering, revising, sharing, publishing—that can help you become a better writer and allow you the flexibility of choosing the direction your writing will take.

The first step in the writer's workshop is **prewriting**. In this step, you come up with ideas for what you are going to write. Prewriting provides you with activities to establish a platform from which you can launch your writing. This is the time to let your ideas flow. Every idea is a good idea and a possible writing topic.

Once you have chosen your topic, you are ready for the second step in the writer's workshop which is **drafting**. Your ideas continue to form, and related topics are added. These added topics help strengthen your writing and give it depth. Depth is important as you will surely cut some of the length during the revision stage of the process.

Step three is the simmering stage. **Simmering** is part of the revision process. It involves putting your manuscript aside for an hour, a day, or longer so that you will be able to come back to it with a fresh objective mind. **Revising** involves you reworking and rewriting your first draft after you have let it simmer for awhile. You are the first editor of your manuscript. Others should help you along the way.

Sharing is the next stage in the writer's workshop. This is the stage in which you give or present your manuscript to a friend, a teacher, or your parents. Ask what opinions they have about your work. Ask them to help you improve your manuscript by offering specific ways in which to change it. Remember, they are just trying to help, so don't get your feelings hurt when they make suggestions for you to change your manuscript.

The final stage of the writer's workshop is **publishing**. Once you have finished your manuscript, you will feel a sense of accomplishment and realize that all the work of writing is indeed worth the effort. This sense of accomplishment will give you the confidence you need to write more and more and more.

Name ______________________________ Date______________

THE WRITER'S WORKSHOP

Tenets of the Writer's Workshop

Put this page in your notebook or portfolio to refer to as necessary.

- Write often and for a variety of purposes and for a variety of audiences.
- Writing has a purpose for teachers and students. Some of the reasons to write are to thank someone for a gift, to share your love for another person, to express an opinion, to obtain some information, to complete an assignment or task, to send a letter to someone.
- Writers should write from their own experiences.
- Writers should use the prewriting step to guide them in choosing a topic or a focus.
- Writers should be concerned first with getting the writing down; then they should concentrate on getting the writing right.
- Writers need to get constructive feedback for their manuscripts.
- Writers need to publish their work, even if that means showing the work to a small group of friends.

Name ________________________________ Date____________

THE WRITER'S WORKSHOP

Put this page in your notebook or portfolio to refer to as necessary. Reread it before you participate in any phase of the writer's workshop. Always keep in mind that the writer's workshop . . .

- encourages an open-ended process.
- liberates writers.
- energizes writers.
- helps make reading/writing connections.
- stimulates the right-brain.
- enables images to emerge.
- focuses on writing stages.
- helps eliminate writer's block.
- captures inner narratives.
- helps you decide what to write.
- elicits a first draft.
- demands that writers edit, revise, and rewrite their manuscripts.
- is a useful technique.
- takes the "fear" out of writing.
- involves writers helping writers.
- helps the writer form associations for writing.
- helps the writer explore natural writing.
- differs for every writer.
- triggers memories to use for writing.
- uses checklists.
- develops out of brainstorming.
- determines a writing plan.
- connects with the writer himself or herself.
- ends with publishing and sharing.

CHAPTER 7
AUDIENCE

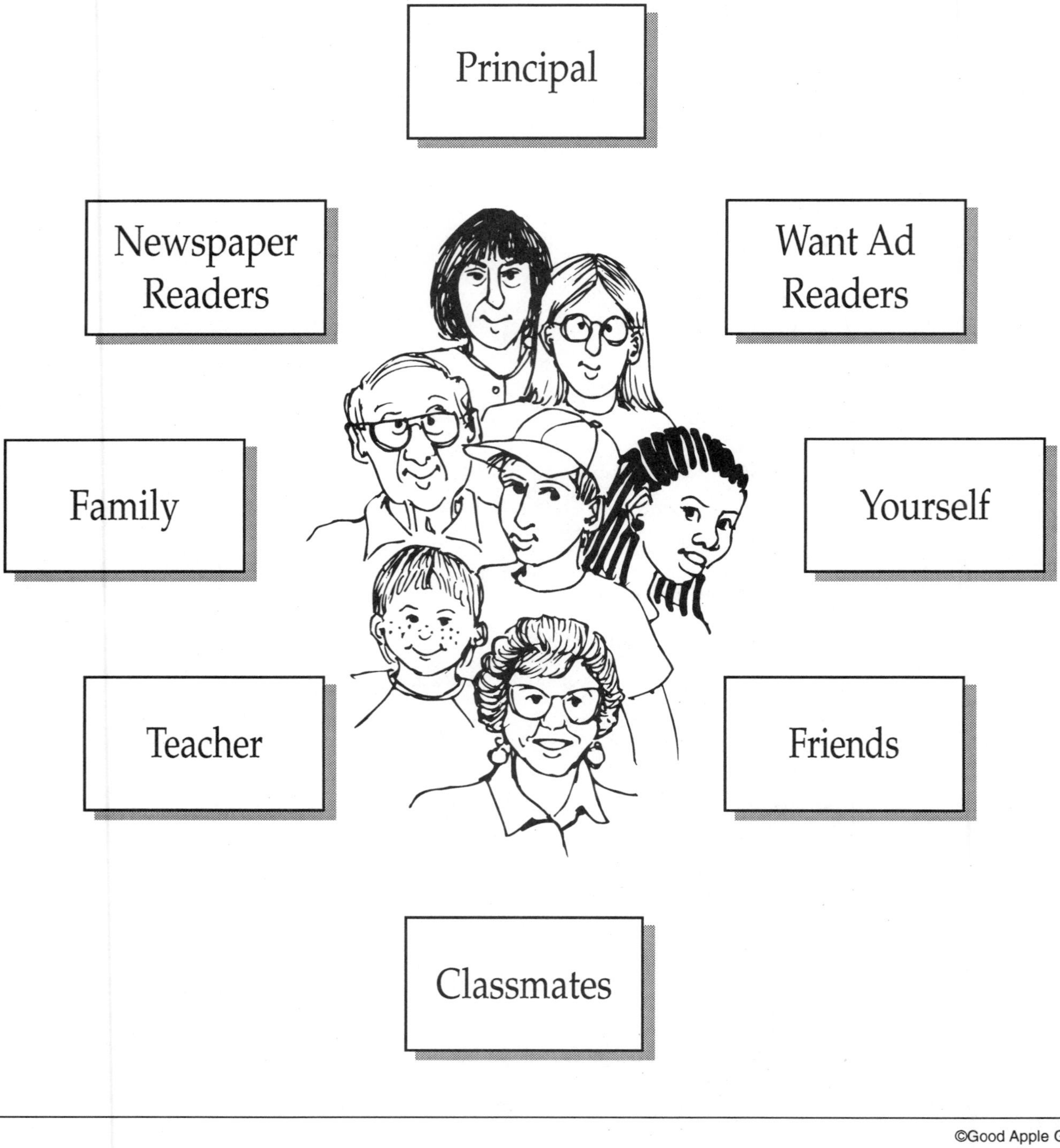

Principal

Newspaper Readers

Want Ad Readers

Family

Yourself

Teacher

Friends

Classmates

AUDIENCE

"A sense of audience—the knowledge that someone will read what they have written—is crucial to young writers."

—Nancie Atwell

The first thing that must be considered by a writer for any piece of writing is the audience. You need to know who will be reading your work—whether it be your grandmother, your teacher, or your best friend. Your intended audience determines the tone, mood, theme, and focus of what you will be writing.

Concentration on your audience helps you decide if the piece should be friendly or formal, serious or silly, thoughtful or frivolous. It even determines the topic you will cover.

Once you have chosen your audience, you need to know what your reader already knows about the topic. If your reader is not familiar with it, you must be sure to clearly outline the terms you use in your story, poem, essay, or whatever else you are writing. For example, baseball terms that are familiar to most Americans might look and sound very strange in a letter written to your pen pal living in Iceland, a land where baseball is not the national pastime. However, by using the right wording, you can make yourself understood by your pen pal, or any other reader, when you use appropriate examples, anecdotes, and analogies, and when you don't use too much jargon. Your job as a writer is to make your audience as comfortable with your topic as you are.

To demonstrate how different audiences might react to the same piece of writing, pretend you want to write an article about street gangs for an English assignment. Many people would be interested in reading about this topic—the principal, your classmates, a local juvenile police officer, the neighborhood director of youth services, parents of teens, and even gang members themselves. Remember that each reader of your paper will read it from his or her own point of view. It is vital, therefore, that you write with a specific audience in mind.

Name ______________________________ Date__________

WRITERS' TIPS—AUDIENCE

Place the writers' tips below in your notebook or portfolio to refer to when you begin a piece of writing.

As a writer, you should ask yourself these questions:

- Why am I writing?
- Who is going to be reading this?
- What are the interests of the audience?
- Why will the audience be reading this piece?
- What feelings or emotions do I want to evoke?
- What message do I want to leave with my audience?
- Is there too much jargon in this piece?
- Is my message clear?
- Is my writing too abstract?
- Is there enough information for my readers?

Name ______________________________ Date ______________

AUDIENCE

In Section One, list the titles of the last five pieces of writing you have done in the left column. In the right column, list the audience for whom you wrote each piece. In Section Two, list the titles of the pieces you will write in the future and the audiences for whom you will write these pieces.

Section One

I wrote . . .	My audience is . . .
1. ______________	1. ______________
2. ______________	2. ______________
3. ______________	3. ______________
4. ______________	4. ______________
5. ______________	5. ______________

Section Two

I will write . . .	My audience will be . . .
1. ______________	1. ______________
2. ______________	2. ______________
3. ______________	3. ______________
4. ______________	4. ______________
5. ______________	5. ______________

Name ______________________________ Date__________

AUDIENCE

Write a letter to your parents asking them to allow a friend to come for a sleepover. Next, write a letter to your friend inviting him or her to sleep over. When you finish the two letters, notice the difference in words, tone, and mood you have used for the two different audiences.

Letter to your parents:

Letter to your friend:

Name ____ Date____________

AUDIENCE

Write a letter to the principal of your school requesting that the school cafeteria offer a larger variety of foods that students like to eat. Keep in mind who your audience is, and, to give your letter authority, be sure to include the main parts of a letter: heading, inside address, greeting, body, closing, and signature. Request in your letter a response from the principal.

________________________________ ← **heading**

____

____

________________________________ ← **inside address**

____

____

body ↓

________________________________ ← **greeting**

____

____

____

____

____

____

____

____

________________________________ ← **closing**

________________________________ ← **signature**

Name ______________________________ Date______________

AUDIENCE

Below is a list audiences for whom you may write. Put a check in the box next to each type of audience for whom you have written in the last month. Continue to check each box after you have written for a new audience. Keep this page in your notebook or portfolio.

- ☐ friend
- ☐ grandparent
- ☐ teacher
- ☐ store owner
- ☐ principal
- ☐ sibling
- ☐ pen pal
- ☐ editor
- ☐ parent
- ☐ neighbor
- ☐ member of the clergy
- ☐ contest director
- ☐ camp counselor
- ☐ family friend
- ☐ mayor or other government official
- ☐ aunt or uncle

Add names below of other people to whom you wrote but who are not listed above. Give specific names if you like.

______________________ ______________________

______________________ ______________________

______________________ ______________________

______________________ ______________________

Name ______________________________ Date______________

AUDIENCE

After you are ready to write and have selected your topic, you must now focus on the writing. When you begin your piece, keep the list below in front of you. It will help you remember the purpose of your writing and establish the tone, mood, and language you will use in your manuscript. Keep this page in your notebook or portfolio when not in use.

When I write, I might . . .

1. voice an opinion.
2. persuade.
3. inform.
4. explain.
5. entertain.
6. celebrate.
7. announce.
8. share feelings.
9. forgive.
10. tell a tale.
11. amuse.
12. unleash feelings.
13. describe.
14. prepare notes.
15. make someone happy.
16. get a good grade.
17. exercise my imagination.
18. create suspense.
19. learn about myself.
20. imagine the future.
21. write an action-packed story.
22. thank someone.
23. teach a how-to lesson.
24. remember people, places, and events.

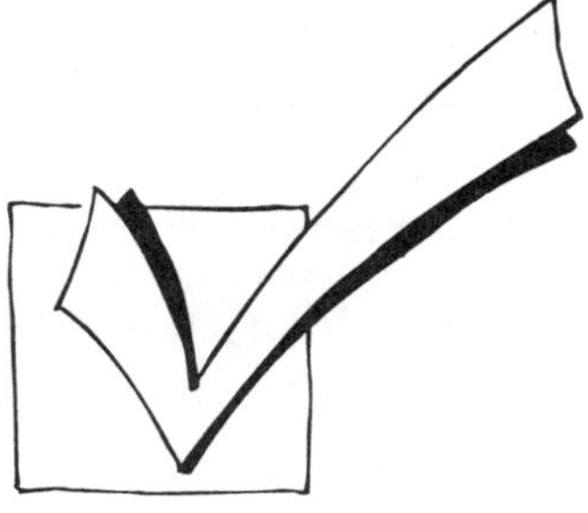

CHAPTER 8
BRAINSTORMING

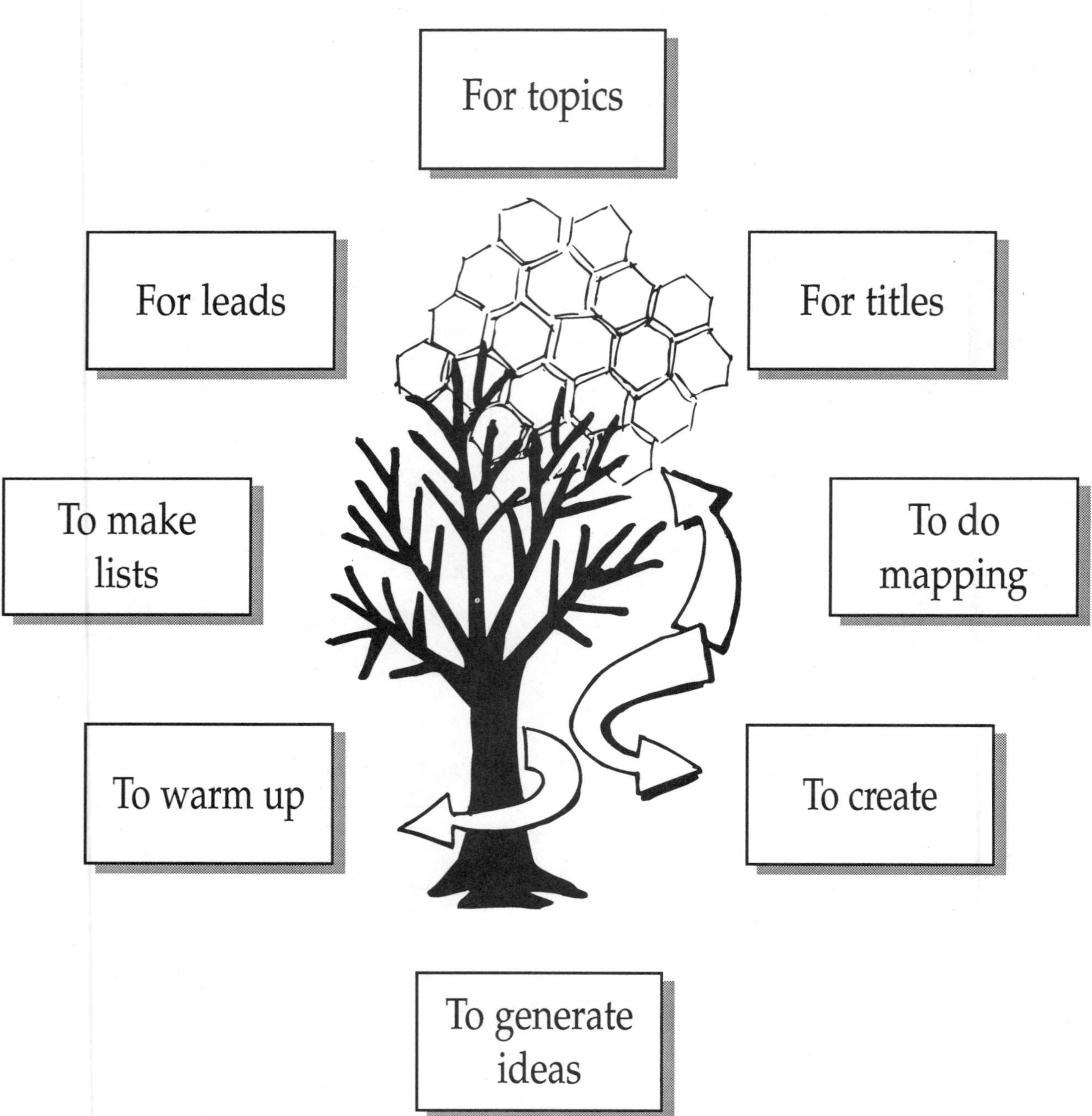

BRAINSTORMING

"The power of brainstorming: no one is allowed to criticize any idea or suggestion that is offered—no matter how stupid, impractical, or useless it seems." —Peter Elbow

Brainstorming is to writers what warm-up exercises are to athletes. Brainstorming is a technique that prepares writers to write. It is an essential writing component that frees writers to begin the process of writing.

Brainstorming begins when you get out paper and a pen or a pencil and jot down a key word in the center of the paper. A good way to keep track of when you begin, end, or abandon a particular piece of writing is to always put the date at the top of the page. Once you have written your key word in the center of your paper, start writing down words, phrases, lines from a favorite song, or whatever else pops into your head or seems to relate to your topic. Let the words find their own connections and associations. You will be amazed at how one word can trigger so many others. Let the right side of your brain, the creative side, take over. Be free, be silly, be sad, be curious, be careless. Just write and write and write and let your mind's eye allow your pen or pencil to spill thoughts and word images onto your paper.

After you have written all that you can that relates to your topic, stop and let your eyes wander over what you have written until something catches your attention. At this point, you might be ready to say, "I know what I want to say. I now have focus. I now have something to write about." However, if, after the brainstorming phase, you are still unsure as to what to write about, draw circles or doodles and scribbles. Perhaps in this way, an idea for what you want to write will come to you. But if you still don't know what to say, don't worry about it. You may just need more time to think about the direction you want your writing to take.

Sometimes brainstorming is called free writing, clustering, treeing, or mapping. These names come primarily from the shape the wording takes—a cluster, a tree, a schema, or a rambling pattern which writers use to help organize their thoughts on paper. No way is better than another. The shape of your brainstorming evolves as you work to put words on a blank sheet of paper. It is not the shape, however, that is the crucial step—it is the process.

Name ______________________________ Date______________

BRAINSTORMING TECHNIQUES

Below are four samples of brainstorming techniques. Their shape is not important. Rather, it is simply using a brainstorming technique to start your writing that is important. On pages 55–58, you will have opportunities to become more familiar with these different brainstorming techniques. See if one suits you better than the others. (Keep this page in your portfolio or notebook to remind you of the different brainstorming techniques you can use.)

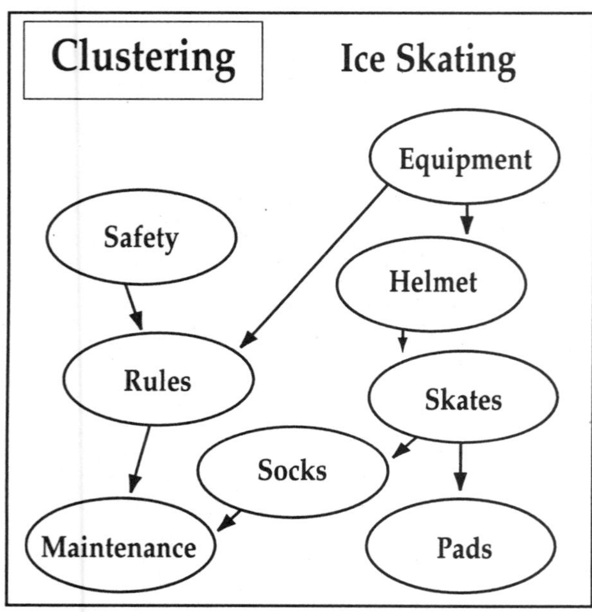

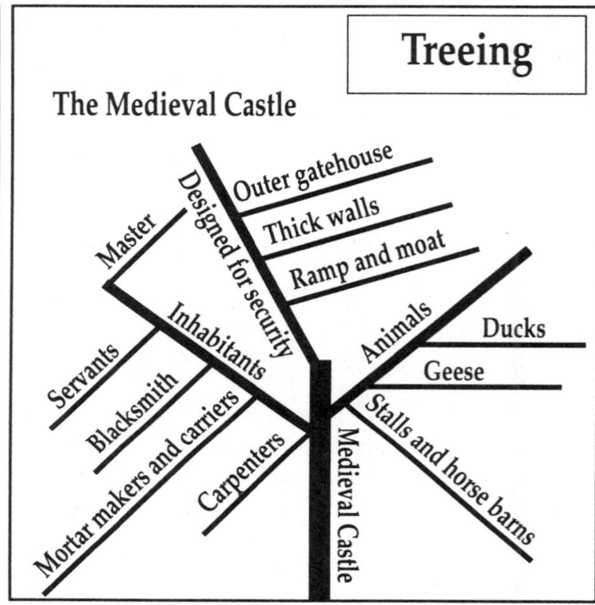

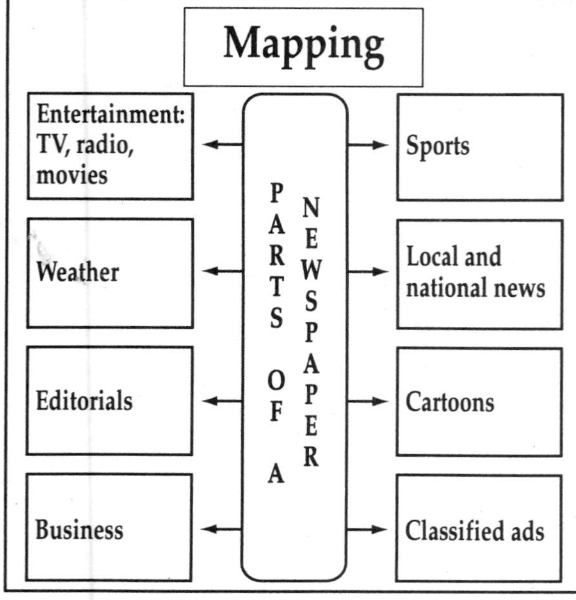

Listing

Michael Jordan

#23	Olympic Dream Team
Athlete	Number of steals
Stats	Dynamite
Basketball	Competitor
Chicago Bulls	University of N. Carolina
Offensive rebounds	Cut from the team
Free throws percentage	MVP
Legend	Airborne

Name ______________________________ Date______________

BRAINSTORMING: CLUSTERING

Clustering is one kind of brainstorming. Look at the word in the center of the page. After thinking about **Yellow** for a second or two, fill in the bubbles that surround **Yellow** with words, thoughts, ideas, and feelings that relate to this idea. You may want to change the direction of the arrows, or you may want to add more bubbles to the page. When you are finished with the page, you might like to write a poem or a short story using **Yellow** as the focal point.

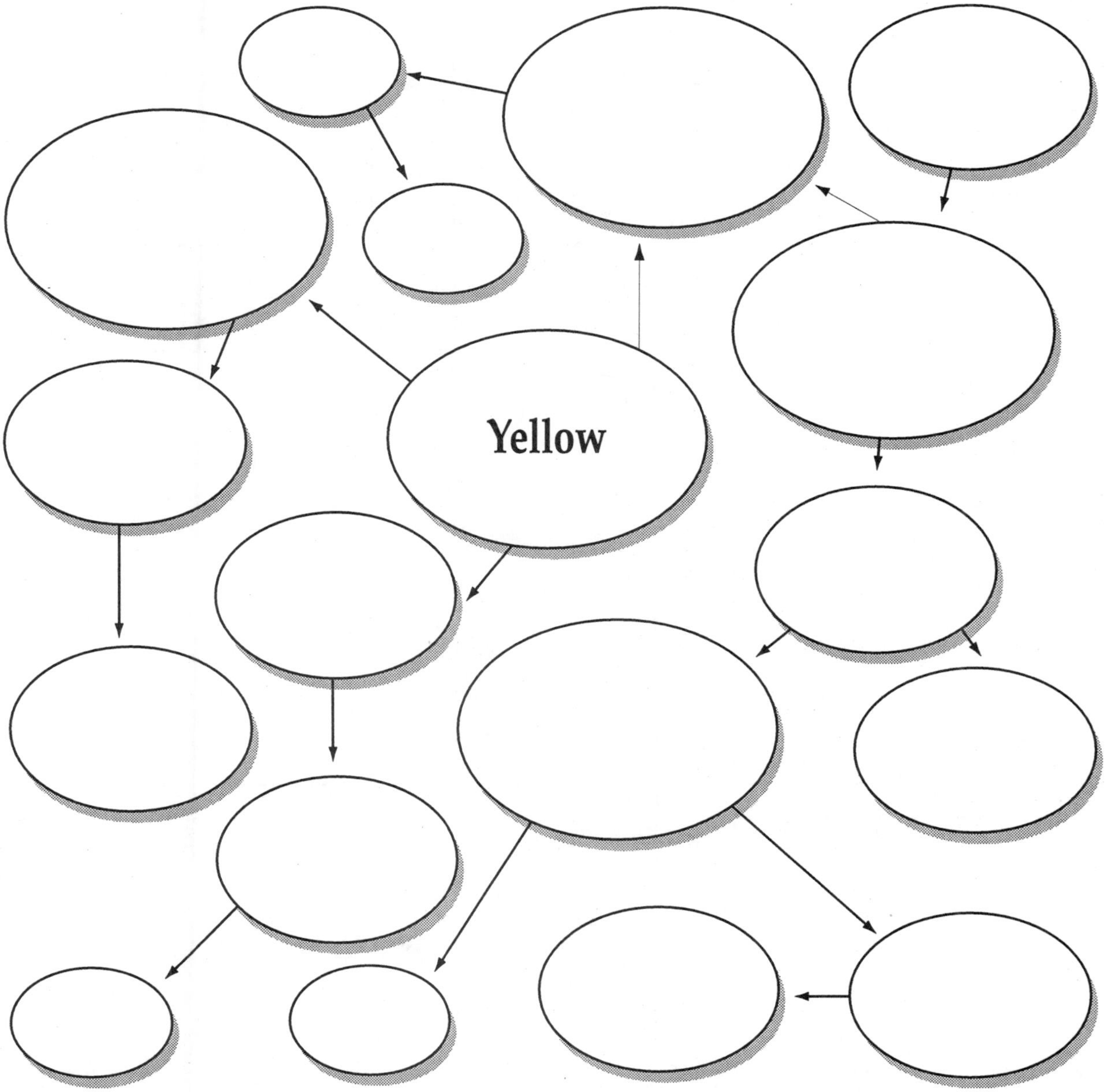

Yellow

Name ______________________________ Date______________

BRAINSTORMING: MAPPING

Mapping is one kind of brainstorming. Write a word in the center of the map and think of as many related ideas or topics as you can. Write them in the boxes.

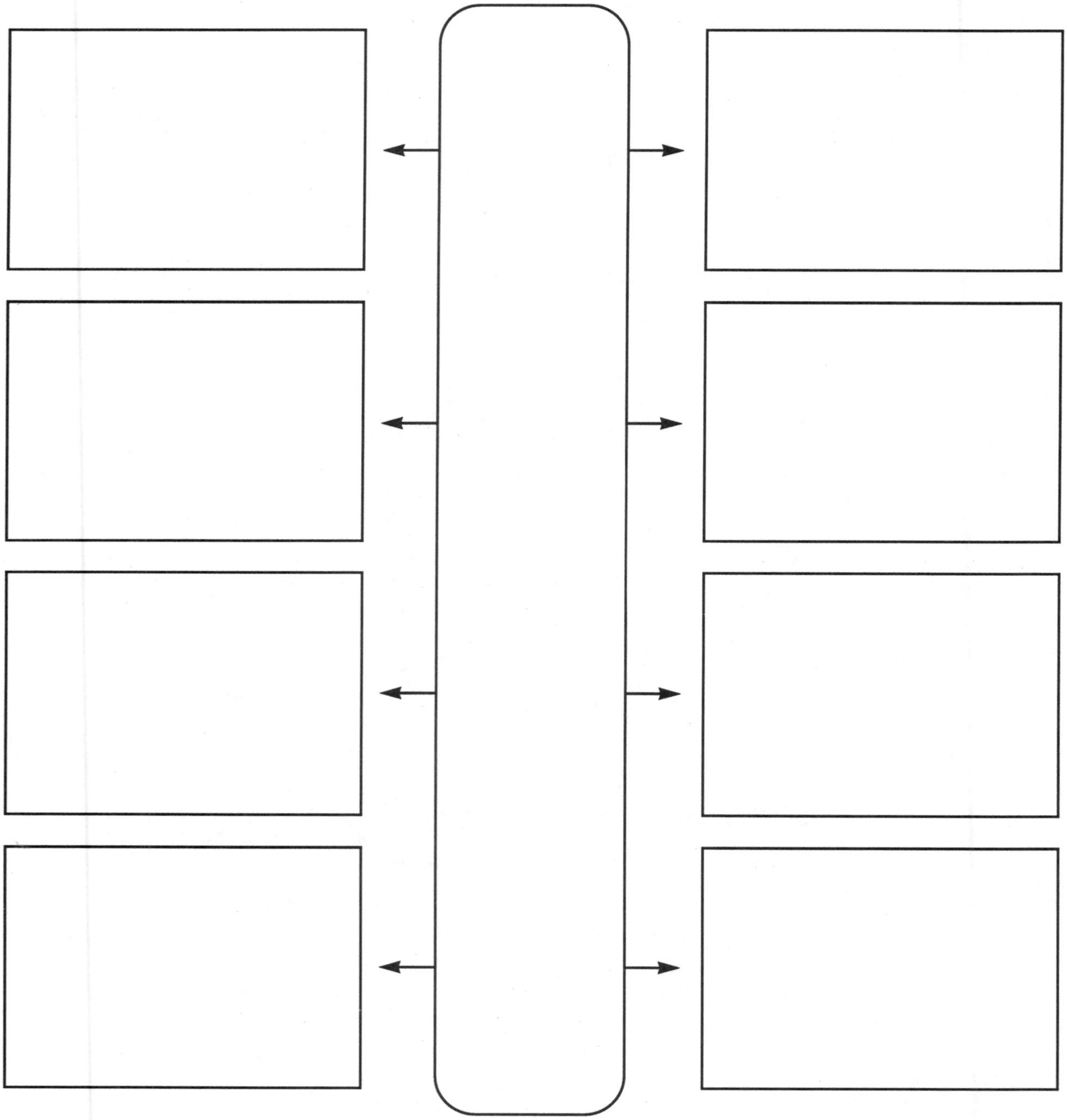

Name ____ Date__________________

Brainstorming: Treeing

Treeing is one kind of brainstorming. Write a word or phrase on the line at the top of the tree. Then write additional words or phrases on the lines branching off the tree trunk that relate to the word or phrase at the top of the tree.

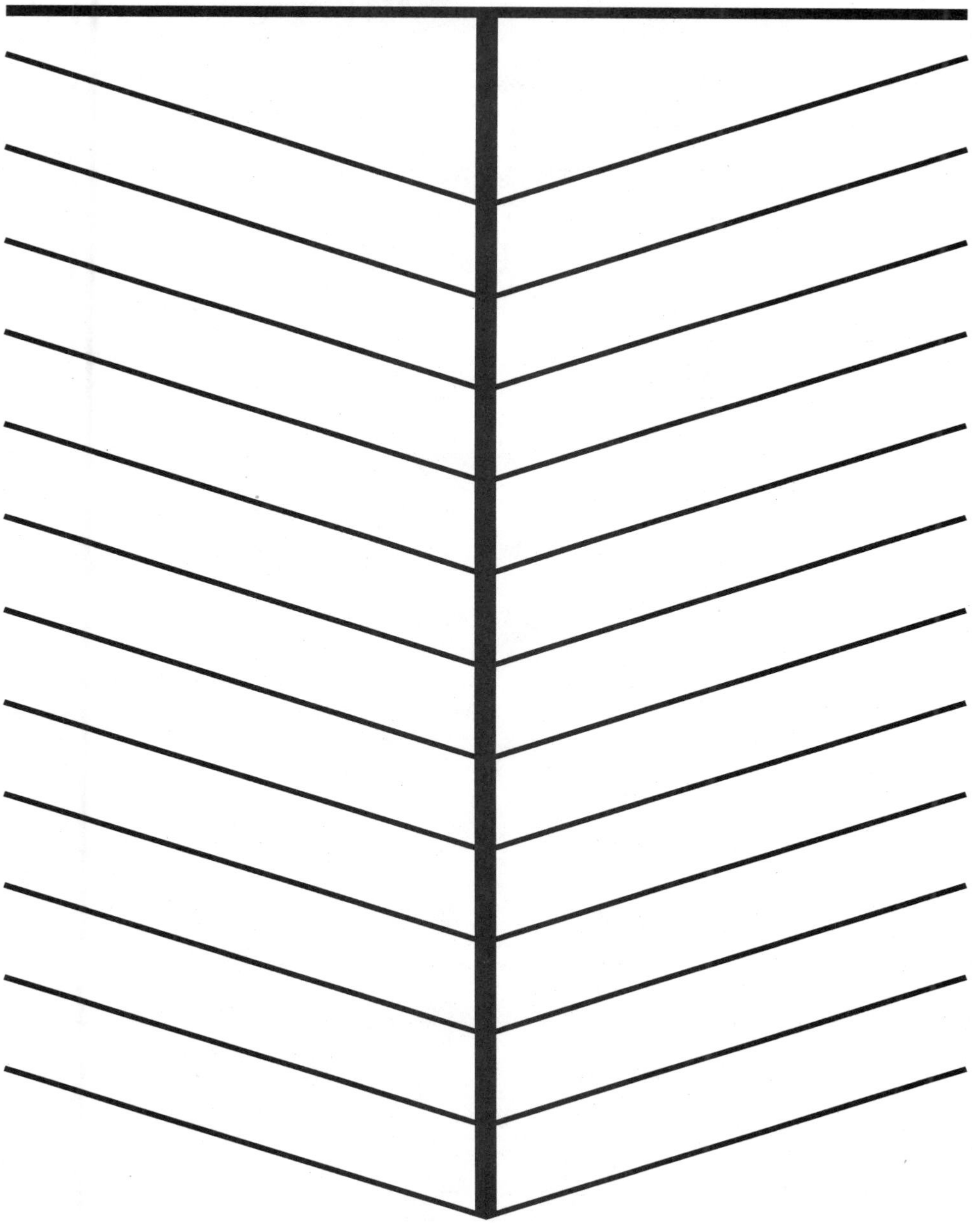

Name ______________________________ Date______________

BRAINSTORMING: LISTING

Listing is one kind of brainstorming. Write a word in the shape at the top. On the lines provided, write down everything that pops into your mind related to the word in the shape.

Name ______________________________ Date__________

Brainstorming Guidelines

Brainstorming is a great warm-up exercise. Use the list of ideas below to get the most out of each of your brainstorming sessions. Put this page in your portfolio or notebook to refer to when necessary.

- Get comfortable.
- Write down every idea that comes to mind no matter how foolish it may seem.
- Write words, phrases, or lines of words from a song that pop into your head.
- Don't stop to correct errors; use the nonstop technique of writing.
- If you are stuck, doodle or draw. This often generates ideas.
- Keep up the brainstorming process for at least three to five minutes.
- Write a word or a phrase, then another, and another, and another.
- Let the direction of the piece unfold on paper.
- Put down ideas as if you were laying down pieces in a puzzle.
- Don't think any further ahead than the next word.
- Keep your hand moving on the paper.
- Be patient.
- Respond to the blank page.

Name ______________________________ Date______________

Brainstorming

Brainstorming techniques are as individual as the writer using them. Listed below are a variety of ways in which to brainstorm and ways of thinking about brainstorming. Put this list in your portfolio or notebook. Over the course of the year, put a check mark in each box as you practice each item listed.

- ☐ Map your thoughts.
- ☐ Cluster your ideas.
- ☐ Select a writing topic.
- ☐ Investigate deeper into a topic.
- ☐ List words from a science topic.
- ☐ Find your way into a piece of writing.
- ☐ Select a kind of writing.
- ☐ Start a letter.
- ☐ Start a poem.
- ☐ Outline a book report.
- ☐ Brainstorm for topics.
- ☐ Brainstorm for a writing slant.
- ☐ List whatever comes to mind.
- ☐ Interview someone for ideas.
- ☐ Make a chart of new words.
- ☐ Connect your thoughts.
- ☐ Create fresh ideas.
- ☐ Respond to word stimuli.
- ☐ Set up a persuasive piece of writing.
- ☐ Explore an essay topic.
- ☐ Plan a research paper.
- ☐ Brainstorm for leads.
- ☐ Brainstorm titles.
- ☐ Brainstorm for current events topics.

SELF-EDITING

Editing should be kept in its place . . . but this does not mean it should be banished from the writing room.

—Lucy McCormick Calkins

Even the most successful writers make many changes in their manuscripts. The first draft of any piece of writing usually contains some errors. They may be minor, or they may be serious. After completing any piece of writing, you must go over your manuscript to correct errors that you have made to try to improve your piece of writing.

Few writers enjoy editing their work, and for many writers, the process of editing is difficult. Editing should begin with you. Look for errors in spelling, capitalization, and punctuation. Look for errors in word usage, meaning, and sentence structure. When you have finished editing your manuscript, turn it over to a peer or ask an adult to examine it. Have him or her search for errors you may have missed. Once the paper has been thoroughly edited, it is ready to be copied as a second draft.

Name ______________________________ Date______________

SELF-EDITING GUIDELINES

As you reread your manuscript, keep in mind that there are many ways to improve your writing. Below is a set of self-editing guidelines. Refer to them during the self-editing phase of the writing process, and paste them in your notebook or portfolio. Put a check in the boxes as you complete each task.

- ☐ Read through your manuscript before you begin to make any changes.
- ☐ Act like a reporter. Ask yourself Who, What, Where, When, How, and Why questions about your manuscript to make sure that your writing is as clear as it can be. It's a good idea to jot down any questions that come to mind as you are reading through your manuscript.
- ☐ Now read through your paper again. Look for specific changes that need to be made. Check subject and verb agreement, spelling, nonparallel structures, and be sure there are no sentence fragments. Use strong, descriptive verbs, and weed out extra words that modify nouns and verbs.
- ☐ Watch out for redundancies. Remember, using fewer words strengthens your writing.
- ☐ Read your manuscript aloud. Your ears will be able to detect flaws that your eyes miss. Listen for smoothness, "right" word choices, proper sequencing, and completeness of thought and meaning.
- ☐ Are the parts of the manuscript in the right order? Are your ideas, thoughts, and paragraphs organized in the correct sequence so as to enable the reader to understand your writing?
- ☐ Is your paper in sharp focus?
- ☐ Is your "voice" loud and clear?

Name ______________________________ Date______________

SELF-EDITING PRACTICE

Edit the expository piece below. You should try to find 14 errors. Look through each numbered sentence, find the mistakes, and correct each one.

When Man Met Dog

1. The meating among man and dog must have took place at almost the same time that man started using tools. **2.** Archaeologists speculate that that was some 500,000 years ago. **3.** They have finded fossils in some of mans early cave dwellings which indicate the presence of dogs. **4.** Actually, the dog was man's first domestic animal. **5.** This relationship soon became a partnership, and early cave paintings show dogs helping men to trap wild game. **6.** It is conceivable that in those primitive times, dogs also stood guard at their masters' caves, played with the young children, and helped carry heavy loads.

7. Scientists do not know exactly how man first tamed the dog, but the most important clue to the answer lays in the nature of the dog itself. **8.** All dogs, even wild breeds, is basically friendly, social animal that have the ability to develop strong attachments to human beings.

9. The Alaskan malamute is a powerful sled dog raised by alaskan indians until it becomes friendly and loyal. **10.** This same thing may of taken place at the dawn of human history.

11. Perhaps a litter of wild puppies was taken back to a cave dwelling and raised in the presence of people. **12.** Maybe a wild dog discovered that sharing the company of men resulted in protection, including easier access to food. **13.** It is a tribute to the intelligence and adaptability of the dog that it were able to take advantage of the relationship. **14.** The partnership proved to be beneficial too both.

15. The struggling human race, learning to live in a harsh environment, found in the dog a loyal protector and devoted companion. **16.** Hunting became easiest; the sound of the night were less fearful—all because of the presence of a wild animal that chose to live with men.

Name ______________________________ Date______________

PRACTICE ANSWER KEY

The 14 corrections are listed below. Did you spot all of them?

- Sentence #1: **meating - meeting. Meat** is food or flesh. **Meet** means "to come upon or encounter."
- Sentence #1: **among - between. Among** is used when speaking of more than two persons or things. **Between** is used when speaking of only two—man and dog.
- Sentence #1: **took - taken** is the past participle. With "have," it forms the present perfect tense.
- Sentence #3: **finded - found** is the past tense of find.
- Sentence #3: **mans - man's** is the needed possessive form of the noun.
- Sentence #7: **lays - lies** means "to recline" whereas **lay** means "to place." *Mark **laid** the dog's food dish near the kitchen door.* **Lays** takes an object—dish; **lies** does not take an object.
- Sentence #8: **is - are.** Dogs **are**, not dogs **is**. The subject and verb must agree in number.
- Sentence #8: **animal - animals** needs to be made plural.
- Sentence #9: **alaskan indians - Alaskan Indians.** Proper nouns need to be capitalized.
- Sentence #10: **of - have** is an auxiliary verb, **of** is a preposition.
- Sentence #13: **were - was** is a singular verb needed with the singular subject "it."
- Sentence #14: **too - to** is a preposition. **Too** is an adverb meaning "very or excessive."
- Sentence #16: **easier - easiest** is the superlative form of **easy**; **easier** is the comparative form for use with two persons or things.
- Sentence #16: **sound - sounds** is the plural noun. There are more sounds than one in the night.

Name ______________________________ Date__________

SELF-EDITING

Use the self-editing form below and on pages 72–73 to edit a piece of your writing.

Manuscript Title ______________________________

Date ______________ Audience ______________

Purpose ______________________________

■ After a quick reading of your manuscript, list the main points of the piece below. Then quickly write your overall reaction of your piece. In your reaction, be specific and be clear. For example, you might react with, "I felt the coldness of the Canadian Rocky snowstorm as it was described."

____

____

____

____

____

____

____

____

____

____

Name ______________________________ Date__________

■ Write what part of your manuscript gave you the most trouble.

■ Jot down some points you would like to have your peer editors consider when they evaluate your manuscript. For example, you might like to know if your thoughts are clear; if your sentences are in the right order; or if you have enough supporting details.

Name ______________________________ Date__________

■ Some technical errors I made include these:

- spelling: ______________________________

- subject/verb agreement: ______________________________

- capitalization: ______________________________

- punctuation: ______________________________

- pronoun reference: ______________________________

CHAPTER 11
SECOND DRAFT

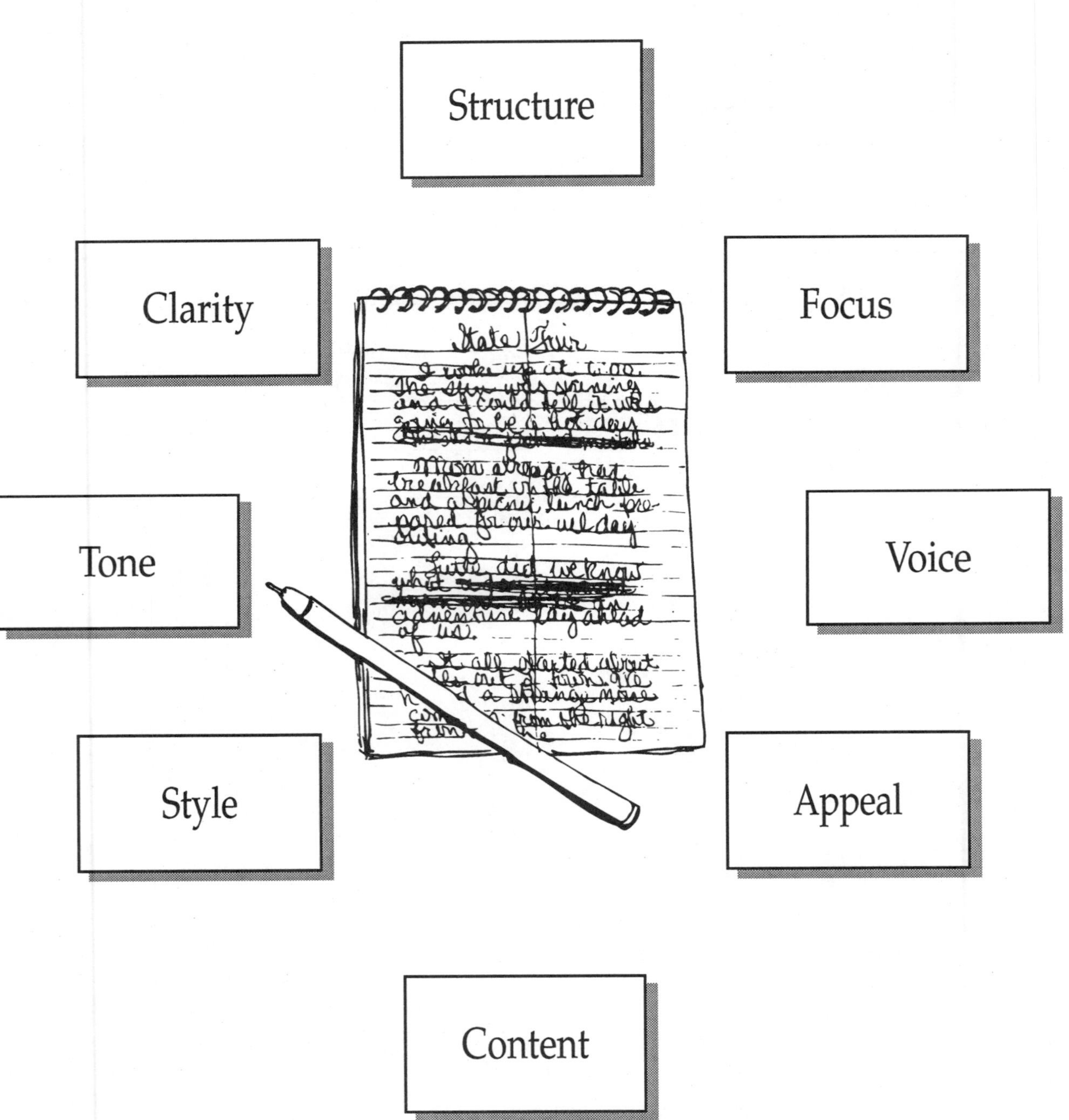

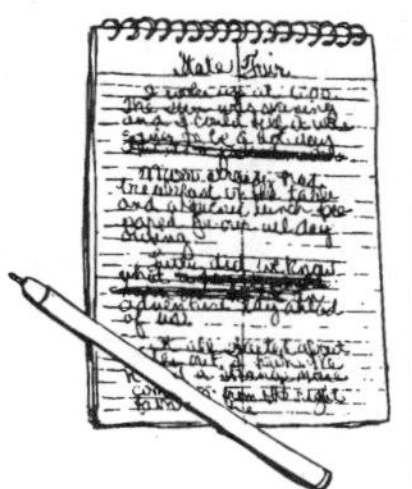

SECOND DRAFT

"The revision itself involves the principles of good editing, the primary one being cutting."

—Kenneth Atchity

After you have written your manuscript, set it aside to "simmer." Then self-edit the piece using checklists, or directly correct the paper as you go over it. Once again, set the paper aside for an hour or a day. After it has simmered again, read it aloud to help you "hear" trouble spots in your paper and to be able to red-mark words, phrases, and parts of sentences that aren't working well and need to be changed.

No one really likes to write another draft, but good, disciplined writers know that this is another essential step in the writing process. You must make yourself revise your manuscript whether you want to or not because you have an obligation to your audience and to yourself to make your manuscript the best it can be.

You want to eliminate as many errors from your paper as you can before you turn it over to classmates or adults to edit for you. You want to weed out mistakes in spelling, punctuation, capitalization, word usage, subject and verb agreement, pronoun reference, incomplete description, etc., prior to giving it to others for review. After you have done this, prepare a fresh copy of your manuscript. You want to present it to your editors in the best possible condition.

Writing a second draft is hard, yet rewarding. The reward of having a more concise, coherent, concrete, complete, and clean paper is well worth the time and effort.

Name ______________________________ Date______________

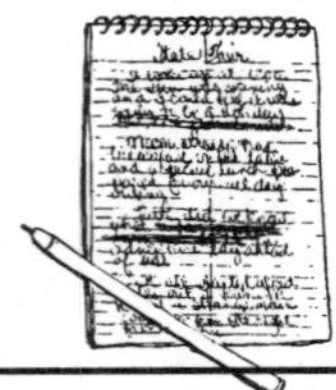

SECOND DRAFT EDITING GUIDELINES

Give the editing guidelines below and on page 77 to peers or parents. Have them put checks in the boxes to indicate where you could improve your writing. Have your editors write on the lines exactly where in your manuscript you made these particular mistakes. Examples of errors are provided.

- [ ] wordiness: "There are *a lot* of people who" **should be** "There are *many* . . . "

____

- [ ] clarity: "Why will *they* be reading this" **should be** "Why will the *audience* . . . "

____

- [ ] subject/verb agreement: "Each *are*" **should be** "Each *is*"

____

- [ ] unnecessary abbreviations: "Dept." **should be** "Department"

____

- [ ] redundancies: "My sister Alma" **should be** "Alma"

____

- [ ] capitalization errors: "kleenex" **should be** "Kleenex" (a specific brand)

____

- [ ] usage problems: "*Their* is a party tomorrow." **should be** "*There* is a party . . . "

____

- [ ] antecedent problems: "Mike lost *her* book." **should be** "Mike lost *his* . . . "

____

- [ ] grammatical errors: "No one had *their*" **should be** "No one had *his or her*"

____

- [ ] useless adjectives: "It is very cold." **should be** "It is cold."

____

Name ____ Date________________

- [ ] missing sensory details: "Jane *walks along*." **should be** "Jane *saunters*."

  ____

- [ ] passive verbs: "The letter was mailed." **should be** "Steve mailed the letter."

  ____

- [ ] lack of use of figures of speech: "The band was noisy." **should be** "The band's sound hit us like a tidal wave."

  ____

- [ ] weak descriptions: "It is warm today." **should be** "The heat swallowed my energy today."

  ____

- [ ] replace words: "By their house" **should be** "By the Adams' house"

  ____

- [ ] beginning needs to be stronger: "I like candy." **should be** "Eating chocolate bars with peanuts makes my mind do crazy things."

  ____

- [ ] ending needs to be improved: "Now I like my family." **should be** "Getting along better with my family would be great."

  ____

The overall strength of your paper is ______________________________

____

____

____

____

____

____

Name ____________________ Date__________

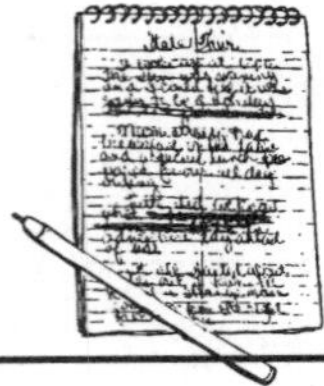

SECOND DRAFT

Write the second draft of your manuscript below and on page 79. If you need more room, continue on notebook paper. Leave every other line blank so you can come back later and edit your writing.

Name ______________________________ Date ______________

PEER EDITING FORM #3

Give your manuscript and this form to a student in your class. Have him or her read your paper and complete this form for you.

Peer editor's name ______________________________ Date ______________

Manuscript title ______________________________

1. Things I like best about this piece of writing are

____
____
____
____
____
____
____
____

2. To make your paper better, I suggest that you

____
____
____
____
____
____
____
____

Name ______________________________ Date__________

PEER EDITING FORM #4

Give your manuscript and this form to a peer editor. Have him or her read your paper and put a check in each box that completes the statement, "I like your manuscript's . . . "

Peer editor's name ______________________________ Date __________

Manuscript title ______________________________

I like your manuscript's . . .

- ☐ title
- ☐ organization
- ☐ ideas
- ☐ use of language
- ☐ facts
- ☐ main point
- ☐ examples
- ☐ use of sources
- ☐ topic
- ☐ format
- ☐ use of punctuation
- ☐ tone
- ☐ accuracy
- ☐ connections
- ☐ supporting details
- ☐ writing techniques
- ☐ beginning
- ☐ focus
- ☐ point of view
- ☐ writer's voice
- ☐ body
- ☐ descriptive words
- ☐ visuals
- ☐ conclusion

My comments about your paper are ______________________________

Chapter 13
Conferencing

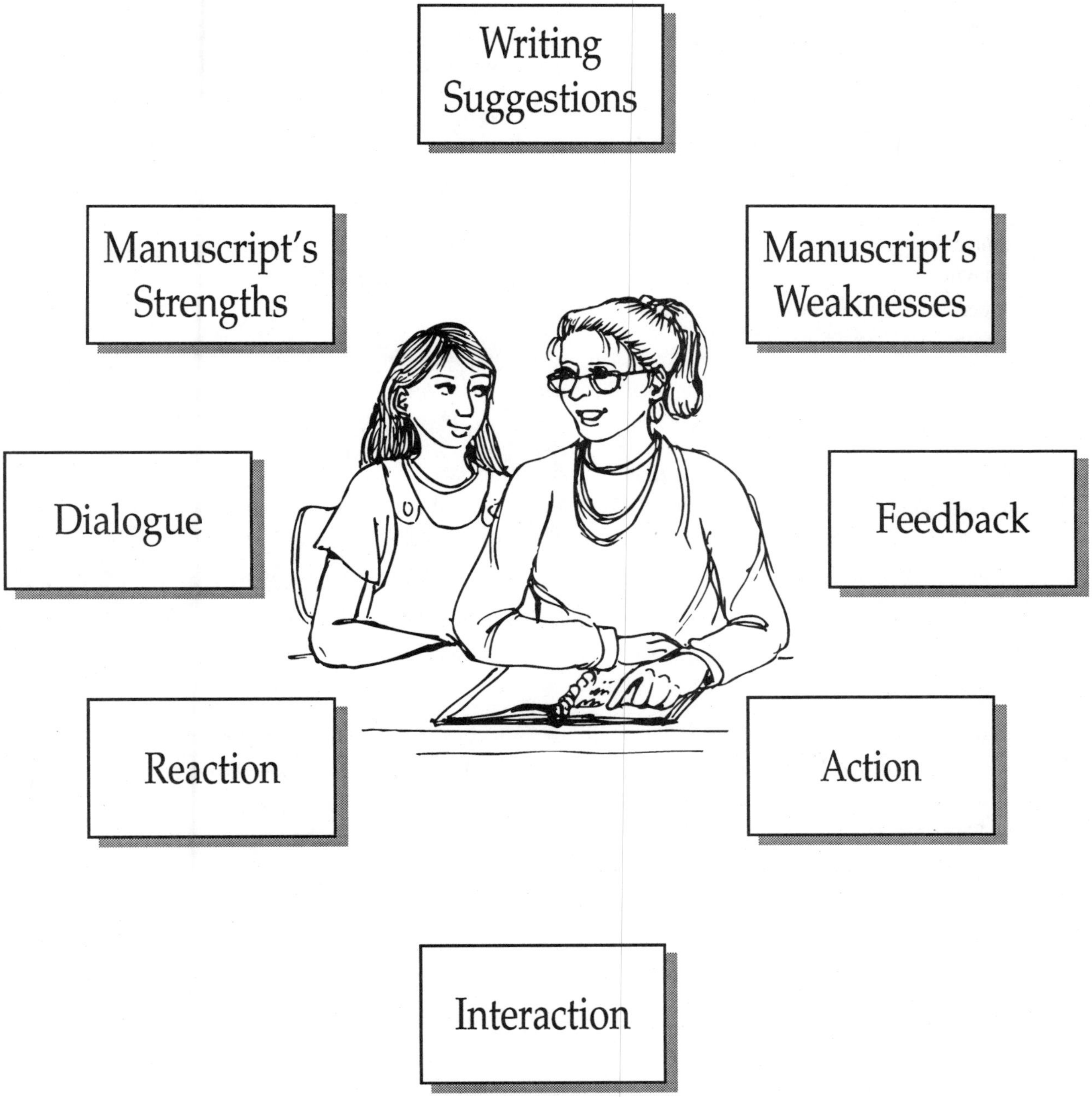

Writing Suggestions

Manuscript's Strengths

Manuscript's Weaknesses

Dialogue

Feedback

Reaction

Action

Interaction

CONFERENCING

"When I revise my first drafts I look for and change certain things. I look for words that are repeated, or scenes that can be condensed and shortened. Once in a while, characters wander in for no particular reason and I have to shoo them out."

—Beverly Cleary

There is no single right way to get feedback on your writing, but getting feedback through group conferencing can be especially valuable. Over time, your writing group will become a cohesive unit. You will recognize each other's writing "voice." You will develop trust in each other's constructive criticism, and you will work together to improve your writing.

Both children and adults learn more about their own writing by sharing it with a group and by asking its members to give specific feedback about their manuscripts. Writing or conferencing groups function best when they get together on a regular basis and when they have specific guidelines to follow.

A simple method for effective conferencing is to have one member of the group share his or her manuscript at a time. Ideally, every member of the group should have a copy of the manuscript to look at while it is being read, discussed, and critiqued. If this is not possible, the manuscript should be read for all to hear, then should be passed among group members for written and oral comments.

There should be a group leader which changes from time to time in order to keep the conferencing members on task. This way, the group will be more effective, and the writers will get more help in improving their manuscripts.

At the end of each conferencing session, it is a good idea to set aside time for each member to express one thing he or she liked about the meeting and then to make suggestions about how the next meeting could be improved. The important point to keep in mind is that conferencing is an effective way to enable writers to learn from each other and to grow as writers.

Think of conferencing as teamwork whose mission is to help one another complete an important job!

Name ________________________________ Date______________

CONFERENCING

Writer and Teacher, or Writer and Writing Group, Activity Page

Read your manuscript. Then complete questions 1–4 below to use as the basis for a discussion with your teacher or with members of your writing group about your manuscript. You can finish question 5 with suggestions from your teacher or from members of your writing group.

My manuscript's title ________________________________

1. The kind of piece I am working on is ________________________________

____

2. At this point, I am finished with the (brainstorming, drafting, editing) stage. ____________

The next step I plan to take with this piece is ________________________________

____

3. The part I like about my manuscript is ________________________________

____

____

____

4. The part I need help with for this manuscript is ________________________________

____

____

____

5. What suggestions do you have for me concerning this piece of writing? ____________

____

____

____

Name ______________________________ Date______________

CONFERENCING EVALUATION

Take this page and page 89 to your writing conference. All members of your writing group should read their papers to the group. After you have read yours and everyone else has finished reading theirs, give your manuscript, this page, and page 89 to one writing conference member so he or she can take a closer look at your manuscript and put a check mark in each box that describes your manuscript. Then he or she should provide you with some specific ways for you to improve your piece of writing.

Conference leader ______________________________

Conference members ______________________________

Manuscript title ______________________________

Evaluator ______________________________

I like your . . .

- ☐ opening paragraph
- ☐ capitalization skills
- ☐ title
- ☐ use of indentation
- ☐ words
- ☐ style
- ☐ sentence structure
- ☐ correct spelling
- ☐ use of quotations
- ☐ edited copy
- ☐ in-depth research
- ☐ thinking skills
- ☐ slant
- ☐ information
- ☐ clarity
- ☐ insight
- ☐ summary
- ☐ topic

Name ______________________________ Date______________

1. To me, the most important thing you are trying to say in this manuscript is ____________

2. My favorite part of this piece of writing is ____________

3. The part I don't understand about this manuscript is ____________

4. When I read your manuscript, I felt ____________

5. You could improve your paper if you would ____________

CHAPTER 14

PROOFREADING

Use of Punctuation Rules

Use of Thesaurus

Use of Spell Check

Choice of Words

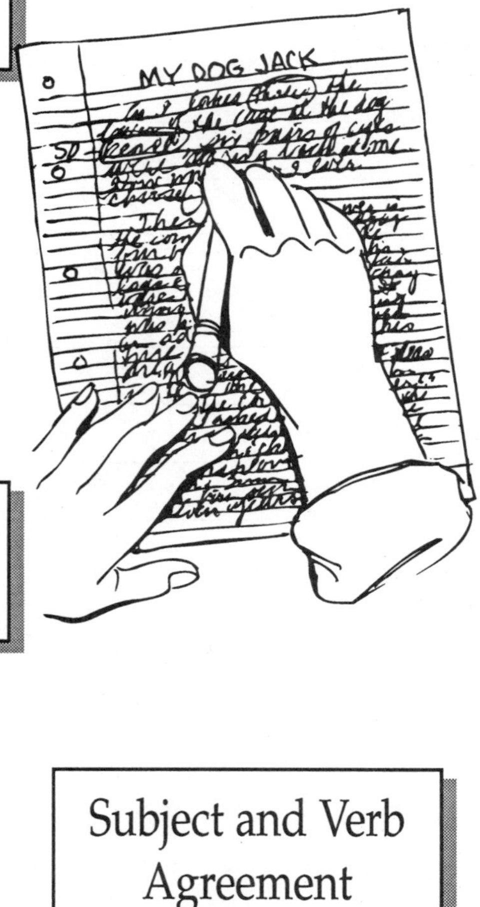

Sensory Details

Final Revision

Polished Manuscript

Subject and Verb Agreement

PROOFREADING

"Express yourself in your first draft, communicate in the second, and make your manuscript sing in the third . . . "

—Eileen Charbonneau

To become a successful writer, you need not write a perfect manuscript. No writer gets it perfectly the first time around. But you need to make your manuscript as error-free as possible. When you finish a piece of writing, it will look wonderful to your eyes, but after some time away from it, you should be able to recognize what is really good with it and what isn't; this is where proofreading comes in. As a proofreader, you need to make sure that the document you have composed is accurate. What does this mean? This means that you have carefully combed through your manuscript to verify accuracy in the following areas: sentence structure, grammar, punctuation, spelling and usage, and subject and verb agreement.

Careful editing will endear you to your audience who does not want to read or listen to writing that is dull or boring, slow or plodding, or full of errors. Proofreading helps you make your writing "reader friendly."

To begin proofreading, read your writing out loud. Listen for awkward words, sentences, or phrases. If, when you are reading your paper, you "trip" over parts of it, this tells you that these areas need to be examined and probably revised.

On your second reading of your paper, pick out specific problems with usage, grammar, punctuation, etc. At this time, force yourself to focus on any vague or generic terms in your paper and substitute specific terms for them.

Next, check to see that you have used strong verbs. For example, did you write "walking" when you were really describing someone who is "sauntering?" These seemingly minor changes can, in fact, make your manuscript much more powerful.

If you hate proofreading, you are not alone. It is probably the hardest part of the writing process because it is difficult, time-consuming, and generally not a pleasant task. However, if you care about your audience, you will do everything you can before you share your work with them to make your manuscript error-proof.

Name ______________________________ Date______________

Proofreader's Guidesheet

This guidesheet should be read and used whenever any manuscript is being proofread. It is a reminder to proofreaders that they should look for common errors which are often found . . .

- near the beginning of a line.
- in proper nouns.
- in long words.
- near the bottom of the page.
- in titles and headings.
- in names.
- in numbers.
- in doubling small words such as *if, as, by, be,* and *a*.
- when one of a pair of doubled letters such as in *omitted, babble, pepper,* etc., is left out.
- when a closing quotation mark, bracket, or parenthesis is left out.
- in confusion of suffixes such as in *typed/types, spilling/spilled,* etc.
- in transposition of letters within words such as in *hutr/hurt, gaet/gate,* etc.
- in transposition of words within sentences.
- in typos.
- in spelling.
- in usage.
- in capitalization.
- in punctuation.
- in not following instructions or guidelines.

Name ______________________________ Date ______________

Final Copy

Write the final copy of your manuscript below and on page 98.

Name ____ Date__________________

final copy continued . . .

Chapter 16
Sharing

Banner

Manuscript

Mobile

Bulletin Board

Poster

Book Report

Oral Report

Diorama

SHARING

"Writing is a public act, meant to be shared with many audiences."

—Donald H. Graves

Sharing your writing with others can be a wonderful and exciting experience. At first, however, the idea of sharing your writing with an audience is probably scary. It is normal to ask yourself if others will understand what you say. Will they think you are a good writer? Will they like what you wrote? Will they attack your writing and hurt your feelings? All of these are natural fears that surface when we ask an audience, large or small, to read or listen to what we have written.

Sharing exposes your strengths and weaknesses, your thoughts and feelings, your vocabulary and organizational skills, and so much more. Yet, most writers want to share their work with an audience, so you must be brave and take a chance and learn to share your writing. Once you see the smiles on the faces of your audience, or tears in their eyes, you will be convinced of the importance of sharing your writing. When your audience enjoys what you have written and shares its enthusiasm with you, you will be energized, invigorated, and motivated to write more and more and more.

CHAPTER 17
PUBLISHING

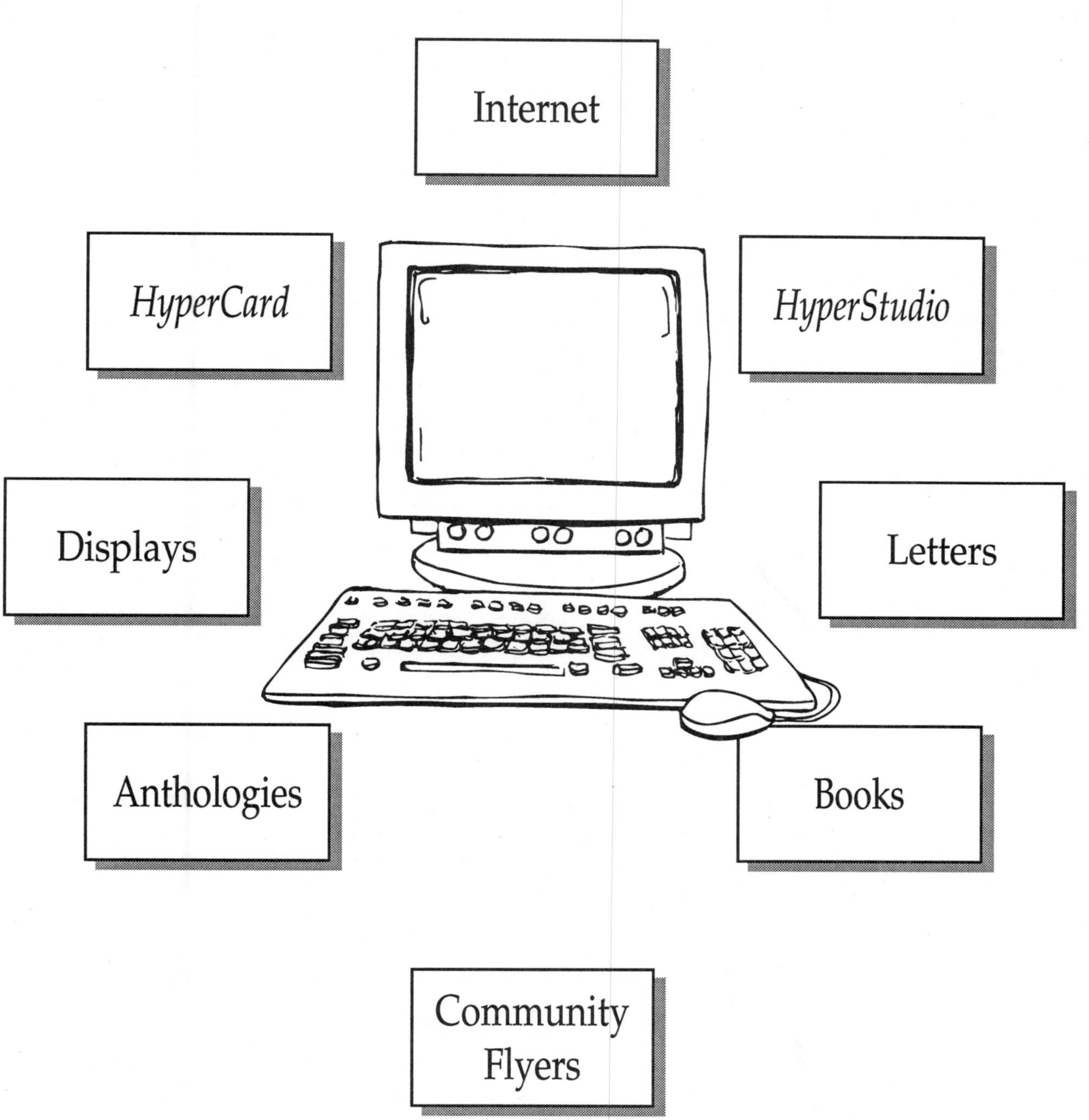

PUBLISHING

"Why publish?" is closely connected with "Why write?"

—Donald H. Graves

When you share your work with an audience, that audience can take a variety of forms—from sharing your manuscript with your small writing group to having your manuscript published in a local or national magazine, book, newspaper, flyer, or the like.

Pages 105–107 contain a list of ways in which you can publish your manuscripts. The list should provide you with plenty of ideas on how to share and publish your writing. In fact, there is an endless list of ways in which to publish your writing, but if you want to pursue being published by local or national publications, you need to send for their publishing rules or guidelines. (Addresses of some of these organizations appear on pages 108–109.) Then you must pay strict attention to their rules if you really want a chance for that kind of publication. Use the boxes on pages 105–107 to check off the ways in which you publish your writing over the course of the year.

Name ________________________________ Date____________

PUBLISHING

Ways to Publish Your Writing

After you have submitted a piece of writing for publication, put a check in the appropriate box to keep track of the way in which you have been published. Try to get published in as many different ways as you possibly can. Keep this and pages 106–107 in your notebook or portfolio and add check marks to them when necessary.

I have published my manuscripts by . . .

- ☐ submitting my writing to the school newspaper.
- ☐ reading publicly before an audience.
- ☐ reading my piece over the school public address system.
- ☐ sharing with the members of my writing group.
- ☐ creating a play or skit and having my classmates present it.
- ☐ being included in a class anthology.
- ☐ sending my writing to a local newspaper.
- ☐ entering writing contests.
- ☐ posting my writing on the school bulletin board.
- ☐ making copies of my writing and sharing it with family members.
- ☐ giving a copy to the local library.

Name ______________________________ Date__________

- [ ] checking publishers in *The Market Guide for Young Writers* by Kathy Henderson and submitting my work to publishers in her book.
- [ ] making a book.
- [ ] sending a letter to a president of a company or to my favorite actor or actress.
- [ ] adding to a bulletin board display.
- [ ] making a poster.
- [ ] decorating the school halls, doors, or windows.
- [ ] submitting an article to the PTO newsletter.
- [ ] writing for a community flyer.
- [ ] being a member of a writing fair or festival.
- [ ] making a bumper sticker.
- [ ] sending a manuscript to a national magazine.
- [ ] putting a piece to music and performing it.
- [ ] creating a dance to tell the story.

Name ______________________________ Date______________

- [ ] writing a public service announcement.
- [ ] pantomiming my work.
- [ ] getting my material copyrighted.
- [ ] making a slide presentation.
- [ ] making a video presentation.
- [ ] creating a *HyperStudio* or *HyperCard* stack.
- [ ] creating a comic strip.
- [ ] putting on a news broadcast.
- [ ] submitting work for the yearbook.
- [ ] giving a speech.
- [ ] designing a display for open house.
- [ ] writing petitions to the principal or school board.
- [ ] writing to a pen pal.

Name ______________________________ Date______________

PUBLISHING

Marketing Your Writing

There are many avenues you can use to get your writing published. The types of markets include magazines, books, greeting cards, newsletters, company publications, and advertising copyrighting. Not all markets accept student pieces, but the companies on the list below and on page 109 represent publishers who currently accept student writing. Keep these addresses in your portfolio or notebook to refer to when you need them.

Calliope. 7 School Street. Peterborough, NH 03458

Career World. The Weekly Reader Corporation. 245 Long Hill Road. P. O. Box 2791. Middletown, CT 06457

Cobblestone Publishing Co. 7 School Street. Peterborough, NH 03458

Current Health. The Weekly Reader Corporation. 245 Long Hill Road. Middletown, CT 06457

Current Science. 200 First Stamford Place. P.O. Box 120023. Stamford, CT 06912

Illinois English Bulletin. IATE. University of Illinois. 294 English Building. 608 S. Wright St. Urbana, IL 61801

National Geographic Society. P.O. Box 63001. Tampa, FL 33663

National Geographic World. P.O. Box 98199. Washington, DC 20090

National Wildlife Federation. 8925 Leesburg Pike. Vienna, VA 22184

New Moon. 2127 Columbus Ave. P. O. Box 3620. Duluth, MN 55803-3587

Read. The Weekly Reader Corporation. 245 Long Hill Road. P. O. Box 2791. Middletown, CT 06457

Name ______________________________ Date______________

Science World. Scholastic Inc. 2931 East McCarty St. P.O. Box 3710. Jefferson City, MO 65102-3710

Seventeen. 850 Third Ave. New York, NY 10022

Sports Illustrated for Kids. Sports Parents. Time & Life Building - Room 408. New York, NY 10020

'Teen. Petersen Publishing Co. 6420 Wilshire Blvd. Los Angeles, CA 90048-5515

Wildlife Education, Ltd. 9820 Willow Creek Road. Suite 300. San Diego, CA 92131

Zillions. Z Mail. 101 Truman Avenue. Yonkers, NY 10703-1057

Name ______________________________ Date______________

GUIDELINES FOR GETTING PUBLISHED

General Information

After you have decided you want to try to get your work published, it is helpful to know some of the general information contained on this page to help you get started in the right direction.

- It is a good idea to consult one or more of the books below for information about submission policies prior to sending out your manuscript. Most are available at your public library. If they are not available, ask the librarian to borrow them for you from another library.

Carpenter, Lisa (ed.) and Roseann Shaughnessy (assistant). *Children's, Writer's, and Illustrator's Market*. Writer's Digest Books. Cincinnati, OH: F & W Publications, 1992.

Henderson, Kathy. *Market Guide for Young Writers*. Sandusky, MI: Savage Publishing, 1986.

Literary Market Place. New Providence, NJ: R.R. Bowker, 1994.

- When writing one of these companies, find out the name of the editor to whom you should send your manuscript. Be sure to spell his or her name correctly.
- Keep track of the date of your submission. Sometimes you will hear immediately whether the material will be published. Sometimes you must write or call the editor to ask about the status of your manuscript.
- If you want to write for national trade magazines or newspapers, send a letter requesting their guidelines for publication. The guidelines will tell you what kinds of writing they accept as well as the format in which they prefer manuscripts be sent to them.

Name ______________________________ Date______________

Guidelines for Getting Published

Below are more specific rules for you to follow when trying to get published.

Specific Rules to Follow

- Send a query letter to an editor to find out in advance whether the editor is interested in receiving manuscripts. A sample query letter can be found on page 112.
- Put your manuscript in the proper form. Most publishers prefer that the manuscript be typed and double-spaced.
- In the upper left corner, single space your name, address, and phone number and type it in block form.
- Your manuscript must have a one-inch border around all sides of each sheet of paper.
- Use only one side of each page.
- Number each page.
- Indicate the approximate number of words in the manuscript. Most computers can give you this information by using the right key code.
- Include a bibliography, if appropriate.
- Follow rules of proper grammar, punctuation, spelling, and word usage.
- Include a self-addressed stamped envelope (SASE) with any manuscript submission in order to get your manuscript returned if it is not going to be published.
- A cover letter should be used when you want to tell the editor something about yourself or your manuscript. Make your cover letter as short as possible.
- Be sure to keep a copy of your manuscript for yourself. Not all companies return manuscripts.
- Send only one manuscript to a market or when entering a contest. Multiple submissions are not necessary or appropriate.
- Know your rights as an author. Many markets assume all rights to submissions whether or not they are published.
- Forms and instructions for registering your copyright with the U.S. Copyright Office are available free by writing: Copyright Office. Library of Congress. Washington, DC 20559.
- Follow all rules exactly.

Name ______________________________ Date______________

SAMPLE QUERY LETTER

Joe A. Smith ◄—— **Your return address and phone number**
514 W. Red Barn Lane
Chicago, IL 60611
(312) 555-5979

May 19, 2001 ◄—— **Date**

Ms. Jolie Jones ◄—— **Publisher's address**
Vendee Publishing Co.
999 E. 45th Street
New York, NY 10017

Dear Ms. Jones: ◄—— **Greeting; Formal style uses a colon.**

Body of inquiry; Introduce yourself and describe your writing. ▼

I am a middle school student at Barrington Middle School. Is your magazine still accepting poems? I have written a series of free verse poems about basketball, and one of them just won first place in the Barrington Area Arts Council Young Writers Contest. I would like to send some of my poems to you for your consideration for publication in your magazine, *Let's Let Young Poets Speak*.

If you still want poems for publication, may I send you samples of mine? They do comply with your submission guidelines.

Thank you.

Sincerely, ◄—— **Closing**

Joe A. Smith ◄—— **Your name, handwritten**

Joe A. Smith ◄—— **Your name, typed**

◄—— **Indicate enclosures, if relevant.**

CHAPTER 18
PORTFOLIOS

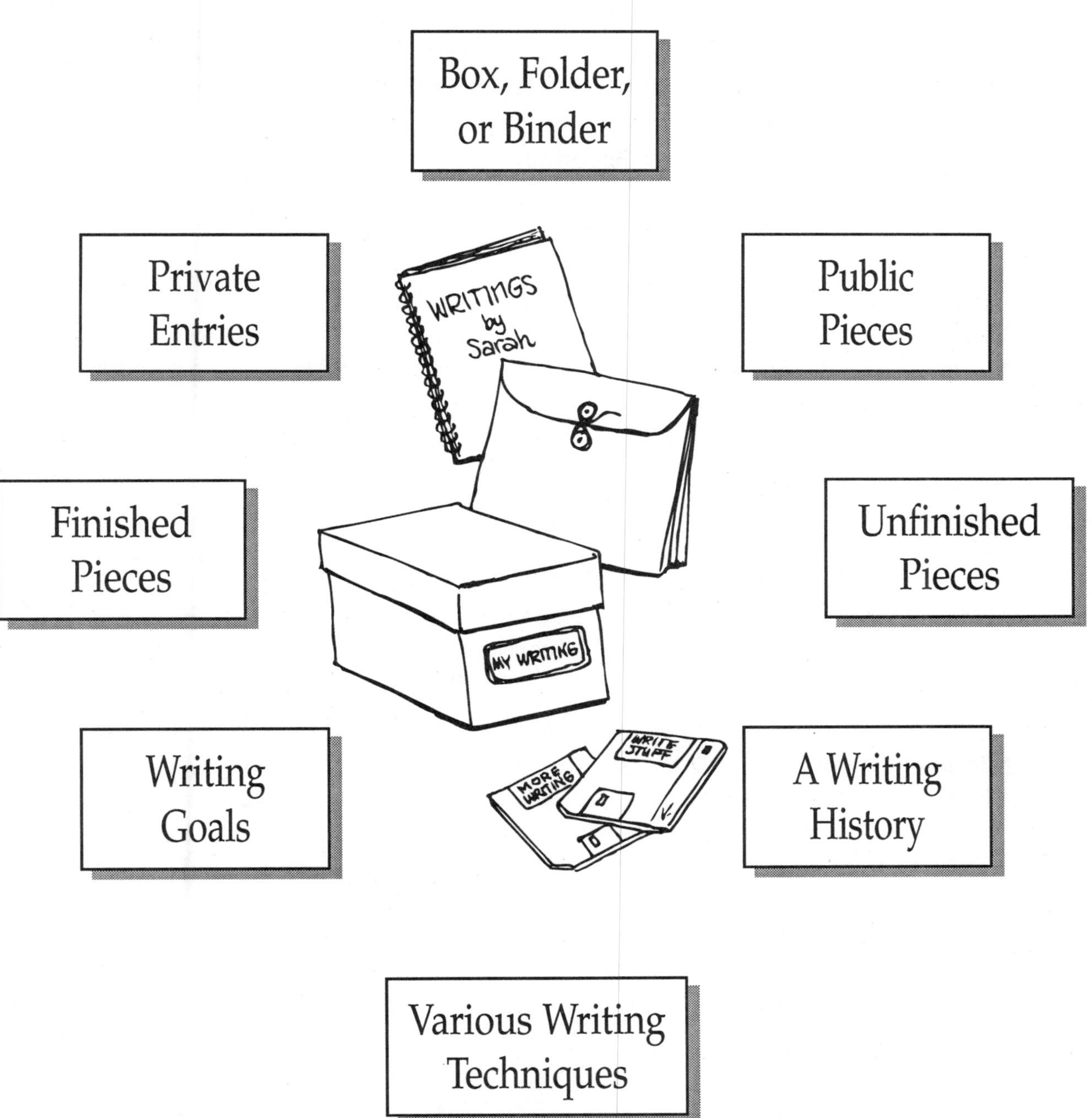

PORTFOLIOS

"Students in my classroom keep four different portfolios of their work: a reading portfolio, a writing portfolio, a technical design portfolio, and a large portfolio for artwork and large project work. If teachers, parents . . . or students themselves need to view or appraise their work, they have a wealth of rough draft and final draft material to draw upon."

—Ron Berger

Throughout history, writers have used a variety of ways in which to both save and publish their writing. Emily Dickinson kept a thousand poems on scraps of paper hidden inside her dresser drawers. Vincent Van Gogh, a French impressionist painter, sent hundreds of letters to his brother, Theo. After Vincent's death, Theo took the stack of letters and had them bound and published, providing art lovers with a detailed insight into Vincent's life.

Writers call their collections of manuscripts portfolios. You, too, should have a place where you keep your writings because they deserve to be kept together and saved. You may wish to store your writings in a three-ring binder, a spiral notebook, a file cabinet, a big old box, or on a computer disk. What should you put in your portfolio? All kinds of writing can be placed in your portfolio. These include poems, plays, essays; copies of thank-you notes and letters; drafts of manuscripts, works-in-progress, finished pieces; writing ideas and story starters; class notes and random jottings; dreams and aspirations; even silly pieces.

You may wonder why you should save your writings. You should keep them for a variety of reasons. A portfolio will let you examine each step you took in the writing process; it helps make you aware of the subjects or themes which interest you. It will emphasize the kinds of writing you like to do; and it can even teach you something about yourself—that is, how you are growing as a writer. A writing portfolio permits you to see the variation in quality and quantity of your writing.

Like writing, your portfolio might have an audience. Peers, parents, teachers, and friends might read through it, so you might like to have two kinds of portfolios—a public one and a private one. Keeping a portfolio empowers you as a writer. You have control over what you put in it and what you leave out of it.

Supported by a portfolio, you will no longer be judged by a single piece of writing. You will also no longer be judged as a writer by one "grade" for one assignment. Now your writing is a reflection of you as a multi-faceted person. Your portfolio is, moreover, the concrete embodiment of you—a writer; a thinker; a strategist; an imaginative, creative being.

Here are some ideas of what you could include in your writing portfolio:

- writing samples
- journal entries
- reading inventories and book reports
- expository essays from science or social studies classes
- notes and interviews
- video or auditory tapes
- newspaper clippings and photos
- letters
- drawings
- writing ideas

Name ______________________________ Date__________

PORTFOLIOS

At the end of each semester or just before the end of the school year, take out your portfolio and use this page and pages 117–121 to assess your writing.

My favorite piece of writing is______________________________

____

because______________________________

____

____

____

____

____

____

____

The piece I like least is ______________________________

____

because______________________________

____

____

____

____

____

____

Name ____ Date_______________

The piece that was the hardest to write is ____

____

because ____

____

____

____

____

____

From writing this particular piece of writing, I learned ____

____

____

____

____

____

____

____

When I compare my newest piece of writing with my oldest piece of writing, I find that my writing has/has not (circle one) improved because ____

____

____

____

____

____

____

____

Name ______________________________ Date__________

After looking over the manuscripts in my portfolio, I can conclude that my writing is ____________

My portfolio is organized by ____________

Topics, themes, or subjects I like to write about are ____________

Name ____ Date_______________

____

My favorite piece in my portfolio is ____________________________________

____

because____

____

____

____

____

____

____

____

The most challenging piece for me to write was __________________________

____

because____

____

____

____

____

____

____

____

Name ______________________________ Date__________

If people looked through my writing portfolio, they would say I am ______________________

I get my writing ideas from ______________________

To get started on a piece of writing, I ______________________

Writing drafts for me is ______________________

I think editing and proofreading manuscripts is ______________________

Name ______________________________ Date__________

For me, sharing with the class or others is ______________________________

____

____

____

I like to publish my work by ______________________________

____

____

____

Put a check in each box to indicate which stage in the writing process you believe you do best.

- ☐ getting ideas
- ☐ brainstorming or getting started on a piece
- ☐ writing and rewriting drafts
- ☐ editing and proofreading manuscripts
- ☐ sharing with the class or others
- ☐ publishing

Name ______________________________ Date______________

PORTFOLIO INVENTORY

Take out your portfolio and look through its contents. Put a check in the boxes on this page and on page 123 for each kind of writing you have completed. As there are many more kinds of writing than you could possibly finish in one year's time, keep the list in your notebook or portfolio for a number of years. Also, the items on the list are plural, so even if you have only one example of this kind of writing, be sure to put a check in the box.

- ☐ ads
- ☐ advice columns
- ☐ autobiographies
- ☐ biographies
- ☐ book reports
- ☐ brochures
- ☐ bumper stickers
- ☐ cartoons
- ☐ descriptions
- ☐ dialogues
- ☐ diary entries
- ☐ directions
- ☐ editorials
- ☐ expository essays
- ☐ fables
- ☐ fantasies
- ☐ figures of speech
- ☐ flow charts
- ☐ folktales
- ☐ greeting cards
- ☐ how-to's
- ☐ humorous pieces
- ☐ *HyperCard*
- ☐ *HyperStudio*
- ☐ interviews
- ☐ invitations
- ☐ jingles
- ☐ jokes
- ☐ letters
- ☐ lists
- ☐ lyrics
- ☐ memoirs
- ☐ memos
- ☐ myths
- ☐ notes
- ☐ outlines

Name ______________________________ Date______________

- [ ] pamphlets
- [ ] parodies
- [ ] personal narratives
- [ ] persuasive essays
- [ ] plays
- [ ] poems
- [ ] postcards
- [ ] posters
- [ ] proverbs
- [ ] questionnaires
- [ ] quick writes (If I were 16 . . .), etc.
- [ ] quotations
- [ ] rap pieces
- [ ] recipes
- [ ] research reports
- [ ] reviews - articles
- [ ] reviews - CD-ROM games
- [ ] reviews - films
- [ ] reviews - videos
- [ ] rhymes
- [ ] riddles
- [ ] satires
- [ ] science fiction pieces
- [ ] scripts - videos
- [ ] short stories
- [ ] slogans
- [ ] speeches
- [ ] tall tales
- [ ] thumbnail sketches
- [ ] TV commercials
- [ ] Venn diagrams
- [ ] videos
- [ ] vignettes
- [ ] writing goals
- [ ] others, not on the list

Other kinds of writing not in my portfolio that I would like to include in it are ____________________

____

because ____

____

____

____

Chapter 19
Word Processing

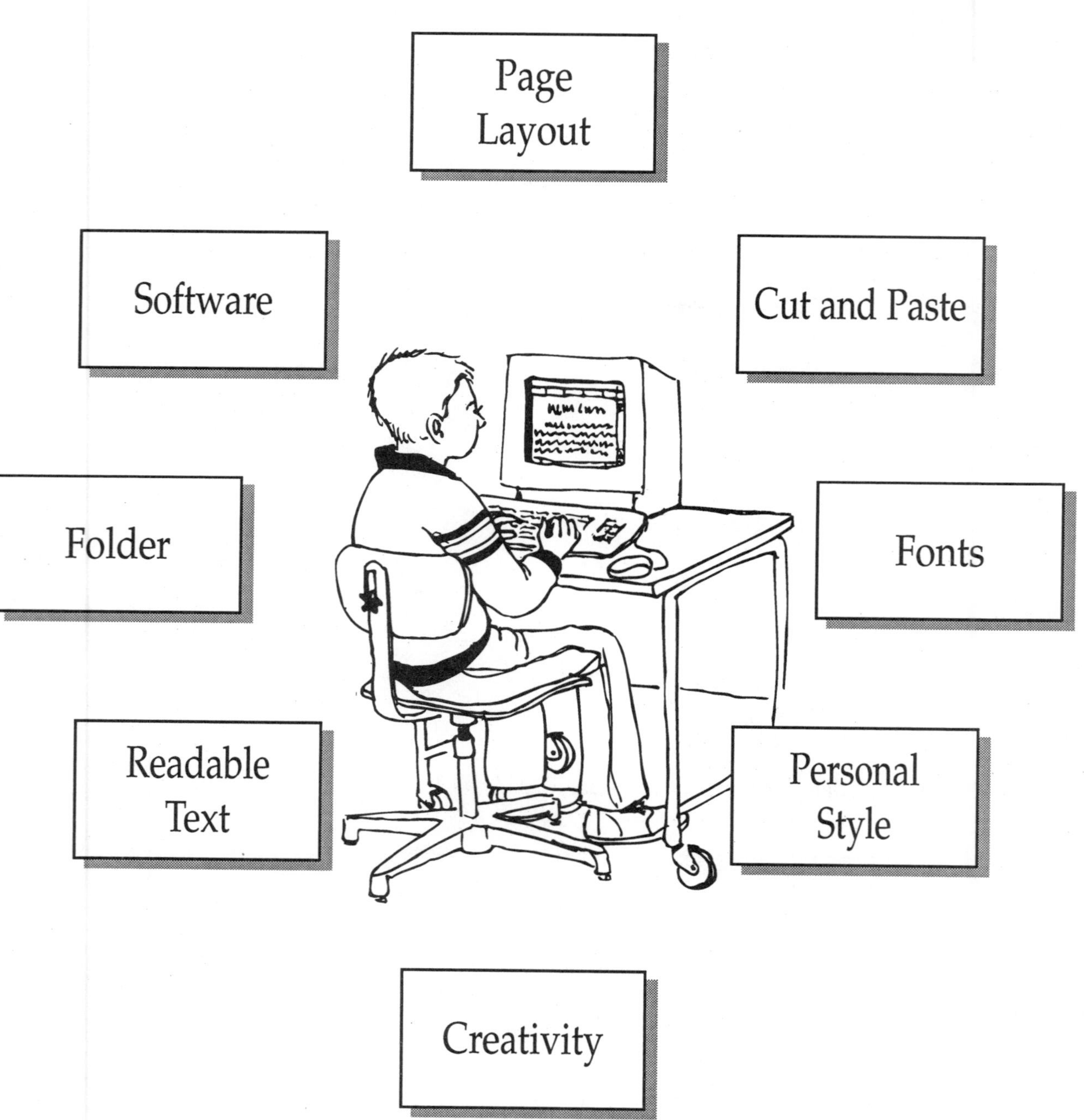

WORD PROCESSING

In a world saturated with technological tools, you need to understand the role of the word processor. Some writers prefer to write first drafts by using paper and pencil. Other writers can be successful by beginning at the keyboard. You need to decide which system works best for you—writing in front of a computer screen or composing in a more traditional manner of using pen and paper. Regardless of how writers choose to write, most agree that nothing gives a piece of writing a more professional look than having the final copy typewritten.

Computers have word processing programs which make the work of writing and rewriting easier. Word processing frees writers from the drudgery of drafting and redrafting their manuscripts. Word processing can be very time-saving, and those who make the leap into using this tool will never go back to doing the business of writing as they once did it.

After you use a computer for a while, it will become a natural part of the writing process for you. A word processor allows you to read your "rights" and "wrongs" as you type them. A word processor also allows you to play with your words right on the screen. You can make instantaneous corrections if that is what you want or need to do.

Computers make the task of rewriting simple because you can easily add or delete words, phrases, sentences, paragraphs, even whole pages, with just a few keystrokes. And since the essence of writing is rewriting, word processors make the process more manageable.

Word processors assist you in other ways, too. They allow you to refine, enlarge, or delete with the touch of a button. In addition, they provide you with a spell check, a thesaurus, and a one-inch, built-in margin all around the border of your paper. Then when you have finished typing and proofreading your manuscript, you can press another button, and the printer spews out a beautiful, clear, clean copy for you.

However, don't expect a word processor to do all the work of writing for you. You still need to physically scan your writing for errors of word usage, letter deletions, and transposed words. And though computers are definitely an invaluable writer's tool, there is still no substitute for careful planning and revision of your paper.

If you don't own a computer and none is available to you at school, go to your local library. Many libraries have computer rooms which house several kinds of word processing programs which you can use. Once you do this, there is no turning back. The joy of writing is now at your fingertips.

Chapter 20

Student Samples

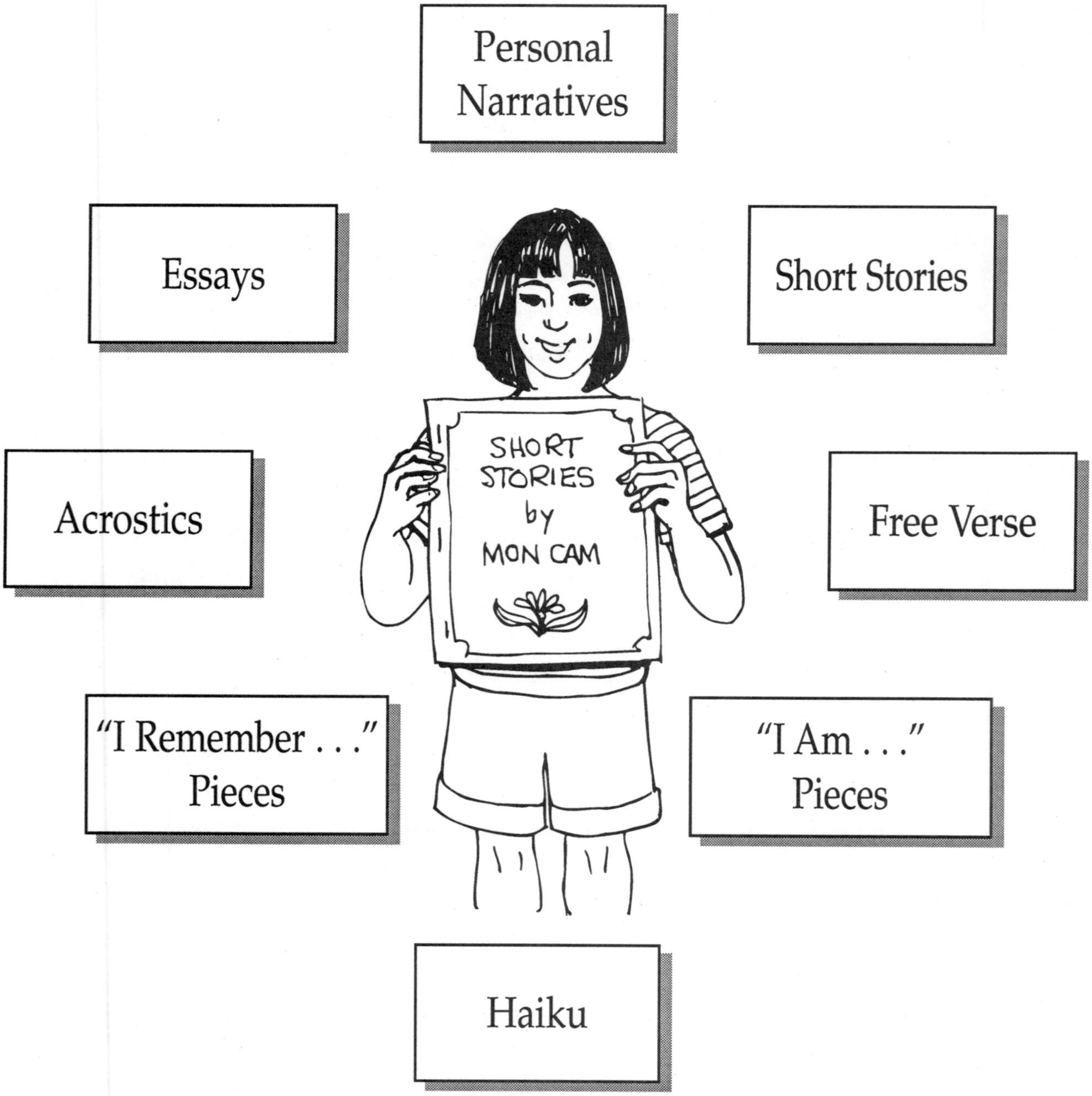

Personal Narratives

Essays

Short Stories

SHORT STORIES by MON CAM

Acrostics

Free Verse

"I Remember . . ." Pieces

"I Am . . ." Pieces

Haiku

STUDENT SAMPLES

"Writing is learned by imitation. I learned to write mainly by reading writers who were doing the kind of writing I wanted to do and by trying to figure our how they did it."

—William Zinsser

Learning usually takes place through imitation. For example, babies watch and listen to their parents and siblings. And over the course of a few years, they demonstrate what they have learned as they speak the language of their parents and mimic their parents' habits, customs, and ways of life.

Writing is learned in the same way. You can learn from other writers. One of the most effective ways for you to learn how to write is to emulate what other writers do. Good authors will show you the way to be good writers. As you read their books, you will unconscientiously absorb their word choices, sentence structure, plot development, sequencing, tone, voice, and style. You can also learn from student-writers by reading what they have written, by observing how they have organized their manuscripts, and by analyzing what appeals and what does not appeal to you about their work.

This chapter offers you a sampling of student writing. Each of the kinds of writing provides a brief sketch of what characterizes it as well as student samples of each genre. Please note that the samples are not those of professional writers. They are examples of actual pieces written by students like you. They have had little editing and appear primarily as they were originally written by the students. So you might see errors in punctuation, grammar, usage, or style, but the core of each sample is presented to help student writers see writing through the eyes of their peers.

After you have read the sample poems, stories, and essays written by other students like yourself, you are given the opportunity to experiment with each type of writing. Read the student manuscripts to see what makes writing work for them. Perhaps you can borrow some of their techniques to make your writing work for you.

Name ______________________________ Date______________

STUDENT SAMPLES–POETRY

Poetry is a bridge of words that connects real people to the real world. Some people think that poetry is only for those who care about blooming flowers or being in love. But poetry is about life. It is about basketball games, a loving grandparent, or a warm summer day. Poetry is about your best friend or drive-by shootings. Poetry can follow strict guidelines, such as the use of couplets written with end-rhymes, or poetry can be as open-ended as free verse in which its length and rhyme are not considered.

Poems should be read silently and read aloud so you can absorb their full flavor. The more poems you read, the more you will notice how appealing they are. Poems by Jack Prelutsky, Shel Silverstein, David McCord, and Judith Viorst are written to amuse us. The poems of Nikki Giovanni, Langston Hughes, Carl Sandburg, and Gwendolyn Brooks open our senses to life in sprawling urban areas. Their poems give recognition to what it is like to be an African-American or a Hispanic and live in our nation's large cities.

Poems are meant to be enjoyed. Authors do not write them for others to dissect, analyze, or memorize. Poems should make their readers see, hear, or feel in a way no prose piece can ever make anyone feel. Writing poems enables authors to give voice to their silent songs. Poems enable readers to feel along with the writers.

There are many kinds of poems. Acrostics, ballads, cinquains, and haiku are merely a few of them. It is fun to experiment with different forms of poetry because you will find that some are easy to write, while others are quite difficult for you to compose.

Name ______________________________ Date______________

ACROSTICS

Below you will find some acrostic poems written by students. Read them once or twice. Then try to write some of these kinds of poems yourself. **Acrostic** poems are written according to a prescribed formula. They use the first letter of a word or message written vertically to express ideas or images written horizontally. Acrostics may or may not rhyme, and the number of lines also varies. Read and see how Kristi and Jocelyn put their acrostic poems together.

Kind
Risky
Irritating
Sincere
Trustworthy
Imperfect

—Kristi Webb

Joyful, jubilant
Outrageous, outgoing
Creative, crazy
Earthy, exciting
Lively, lovable
Youthful
Nice, nuisance

—Jocelyn Bletzinger

Name ____________________ Date__________

An Awesome Acrostic

Now it's your turn to write an acrostic. You may use your first or last name; you may use any other word you'd like. Write the letters of the word you want to use for your acrostic in the boxes. Then write the words or phrases that convey your message on the lines next to the boxes. On another piece of paper, you can add more boxes or lines if you need to.

Name ______________________________ Date______________

Phrase Completion Poems

Another kind of poem you can write is a **phrase completion** poem. It is a poem for which you are given an open-ended phrase and you complete the idea by writing lines of poetry that are inspired by the incomplete phrase. Examples of phrase completion beginnings are "I believe . . .", "I love . . .", "I know . . .", and "My favorite friend is . . .". These poems give you lots of freedom to express your thoughts and feelings. Read the samples and then try one of your own.

I Like . . .
the bright golden sun.
wild, fun colors.
deep, purple grapes.
bright red apples.
young wild horses.
dark pink sunsets.
golden yellow sunrises.
the green grass of spring.
icy, cold winter.
white, cotton-ball clouds.
fast-paced dancing.
lightning-fast tennis.
the wind whipping through my hair.
blinding, white, new-fallen snow.
pale, spraying waterfalls.
swimming in dark blue oceans.
hearing the crashing of the surf.
the silver moon.
the joy of success.
harsh, rugged mountains.
infinite powder-blue oceans.
the brightest time of day—midday.
the darkest time of night—midnight.
yummy, sticky candy.
white hot happiness.
doing jumps on my figure skates.
dark red strawberries.
living, learning, thinking.
—Hermioni Zouridis

Name ______________________________ Date______________

Below and on page 133 are two more phrase completion poems that have the format, "I remember . . ." as their focus. You could read, enjoy, and model your phrase completion poems after these.

I Remember . . .

I remember what he said to me
that dark and dreary day
I remember what I thought right then
That we would always stay
I remember how I missed him so
When he was taken away
I remember how I, too, wanted to go
So he wouldn't be all alone
I remember the emotion in his eyes
When he was happy as could be
I remember the skies so blue
In his hospital room
I remember how much he meant to me
And how much we shared
I remember what he said to me
That he would always care
I remember how I cried that day
I felt my heart would split in two
I remember how I hurt inside
And how everything seemed so blue
I remember the flowers
That covered his grave
I remember the long, lonely hours
Highlighted with calls of sympathy
I remember the bottles of pills
That cluttered his bedside table
I remember how he read to me
My favorite was a well-known fable
But most of all
I remember a most meaningful thing
I remember what he said to me
that dark and dreary day

—Amee Lakhani

Name ______________________________ Date______________

I Remember . . .

I remember times of long, lost loves
And times of long, lost hates.
I remember riding a two-wheel bike
And learning to roller skate.
I remember falling many times,
But mostly picking myself up.
I remember my old sandbox
And my little pup.
And growing fast and hopping too,
And running, playing at the zoo.
Baseball, basketball, football, soccer;
Not being able to open my locker.
Wishing, praying upon a star;
Hoping to get very far.
Music could move me and sweep me away,
Or make me depressed all through the day.
I remember feeling exactly that way,
Feeling the music through my veins.
And stars 'n' stripes,
Fruit not yet ripe,
Laughing, giggling, crying too,
Nothing anyone could do.
I remember summers, lots of them.
Winters cold and white,
Spring flowers and young deer,
Autumns full of Halloween fear.
I remember Christmas time,
New Years come and gone again,
St. Patrick's and Valentine's went too quick,
Fourth of July, times of remembrance for our warriors.
I remember them shady, gray.
I remember the good,
I remember the bad,
I remember the hardship, but won't take it back.
I remember what brought me here.

—Stacey Sajpel

Name ______________________________ Date__________

My Own Phrase Completion Poem

Use one of the three suggested beginnings below to write a phrase completion poem on the lines provided. If you prefer, make up your own beginning for your poem.

- I like . . .
- I remember . . .
- I am . . .

____

Title

Name ______________________________ Date______________

FREE VERSE POEMS

Another kind of poem is known as **free verse**. These are poems that have a regular rhythm and sound somewhat like conversations. Topics for these poems are as varied as the poets who write them. Below and on page 136 is an example of a free verse poem. After reading and rereading the poem, write one of your own on any topic.

One of the easiest ways to begin writing poems is to write one about yourself. These kinds of poems simply start with an answer to the question: Who am I? Lindsay elected to use some rhyme in her Who Am I? free verse poem. You should not feel that you need to make the lines of your poem rhyme. But you might enjoy reading Lindsay's unique look at who she is through the poem she wrote when given this assignment.

Who Am I?

In the beginning,
there were none.

Then one, a boy,
came forth.

He alone was taken,
taken from all he loved.

Then again a boy,
he survived the first test.

But he, too, was taken,
taken from all he loved.

No more
was thought of children.

Later, as time passed,
Still questioning

Still uncertain,
The third boy came forth.

They won this boy,
He came into their hearts.

Name ______________________________ Date______________

Nervous and tense,
They too entered his heart.

But all is lost, he has joined the two,
taken from all he loved.

Lost in uncertainty, an unknown girl,
tried the test.

She will never be ours,
for we have lost three.

She unlike the three,
was free.

Cheerful, lively,
the fourth was theirs.

Then a fifth,
was thought to be.

Another girl,
like the fourth, full of life.

Loved in spirit,
yet not even there.

The girl was taken to join the three,
no more was logical.

The sound of crying,
she was free.

I am the fifth of two,
there are no longer five.

Three have gone,
their ashes lay by the water's edge.

Will I, the fifth, join,
and leave only one?

I being two of five,
see and hear three.

In the beginning,
there were none.

—Lindsay Piegza

Name ______________________________ Date__________

Who Am I? Essays

Your Who Am I? poem can also be written as an essay as seen in the student sample below.

Who Am I?

In 1984, my family moved from Highland Park to Barrington. I was four years old. My mom wanted to enroll my sister and me in an arts studio. So my mom looked into a dance studio and started us both in ballet. This was my first experience in dance.

As the years passed, I started new dance classes and by the third grade I was in jazz, tap, ballet, and acrobatics. This meant that I would be in six separate dance scenes in the annual dance studio recital that was held each spring. That would mean an incredible amount of preparation. Many hours went into getting ready for our performances to be at the large Hemmens Hall in Elgin, Illinois, a community not far from Barrington.

In sixth grade, I decided to try out for a dance company and had to display my skills in ballet, jazz, and tap. I also had to be good. My dance teacher put me in the lowest group of three because of my young age. I was really excited to have been accepted into this company. After three months of rehearsals, we went to competition and placed second. We also went to a workshop. It was hard work, but it was also a lot of fun.

In seventh grade, I started pointe. That's when I found out that I have an extra bone in each foot. I had to see a physical therapist and learn to do exercises so that my feet wouldn't hurt when I practiced or danced on my toes.

I'm learning how to cope with the pain so that I can stay in dance, I also have to manage my time well so that I have time for my other after school activities, and of course homework. Dance is one of the things that has changed my life, it now is one of the things that defines who I am.

—Johanna Ware

Name ______________________________ Date______________

Gender Poems

Another topic that interests writers and readers is the opposite sex and how we view each other. The poems below and on page 139 were written by students after listening to different songs from the record album *Marlo Thomas and Friends: Free To Be . . . You and Me.* After reading these poems and thinking about what it means to be male or female, try writing a poem about the subject of gender.

Boys and Girls

Boys are supposed to be
tough,
strong,
and love sports.
But what if a boy were to
take ballet,
dislike sports,
or play with dolls.
Would he get teased?
Would people not like him anymore?
Or if a girl were to
play football,
beat people up,
or lift weights.
What would happen to her?
Would other girls ignore her
and not play with her?
Why can't boys and girls
just be themselves?
To have people like them
for who they are,
not for what they like?

—Ryan Ball

Name ______________________________ Date______________

Boys

Boys like to run.
Boys like to climb.
Boys like to have fun.
All of the time.
Sports are a passion.
That is true.
Football, baseball,
Basketball too!
Music is cool
To boys all around.
Blasting their stereos
To hear the sounds.
Boys work out
All of the time
To get their muscles
Nice and prime.
Boys are active
And rarely slow down
Skiing the slopes
And blading to town.
Boys are different
They're one of a kind.
They grow up to be men,
But they're still boys inside.

—Blake Holcomb

Name ______________________ Date ____________

My Gender Poem

Try writing your own gender poem. Begin with the word *male, boy, female,* or *girl* and see what thoughts, feelings, and ideas you can come up with for your own gender poem.

____

Title

Name ______________________________ Date__________

Seasonal Poems

From the ancient Greeks to modern day poets, the seasons offer poets endless possibilities to write about. Everyone seems to have a favorite season. What's yours? This might be the starting place for you to write a seasonal poem. Another way to begin a seasonal poem is to make a list of all the images that come to mind when you think of each of the seasons.

Jun Kim began his seasonal poem with the Who Am I? theme, but then put the focus on fall.

Fall Poetry Festival

Who am I?
You have no doubt.
Where am I?
From clues you will find out.
I see leaves, flowers, a grass down here,
A quick squirrel, and a fawn with a deer.
I see people playing wild games as I
  watch with care,
A massive sun, a flock of birds, and a
  cloud up there.
I hear birds up in the trees chirping very
  loud,
Athletes cheering and yelling when they
  are proud.
I hear little kids run around as they tease,
Trees swaying back and forth from a light
  breeze.
I feel the damp, dead leaves beneath my
  bare feet,
The warm sun as it produces heat.
I feel the sticks and stones hidden in the
  grass,
A fragile Frisbee I caught from my dad's
  pass.
I smell the moist ground as I go up a hill,
The sweet barbecue cooking on a grill.
I smell the pine trees so close like
  wanting to meet.
I start to get hungry, and I am ready to
  eat.
I taste the tender B.B.Q. in my mouth.
I swallow and the barbecue goes south.
I drink the cold Coke, as thirsty as a bull.
As I finish my dinner, I suddenly get full.
I feel cheerful, excited, playful and
  happy.
There were many things to feel, taste,
  smell, hear, and see.
The sun goes down, and it turns dark.
Where am I? Where am I?
I am at an amusement park.
This was a fascinating event for me, and I
  must recall,
This is not winter, summer, nor spring,
  but it is simply fall.

—Jun Kim

Name ____ Date________________

Below is another seasonal poem. This poem by James Downey expresses his feelings for the life-awakening season of spring.

Spring Is Here

Spring is here.
It finally has come.
The birds, the trees, the flowers, the fun.

The flowers are blooming,
as fast as can be.
The trees are budding
and falling on me.

Vivid yellows, light pinks, dark red,
all in spring.
Buds, seeds, trees,
everything.

The leaves grow.
The rain flows,
It only stays awhile,
and then it goes.

After spring comes fall.
The mud, the rain,
the slips, them all.

But spring is spring,
not like any other.

It's here right now,
and I'm enjoying it together.

—James Downey

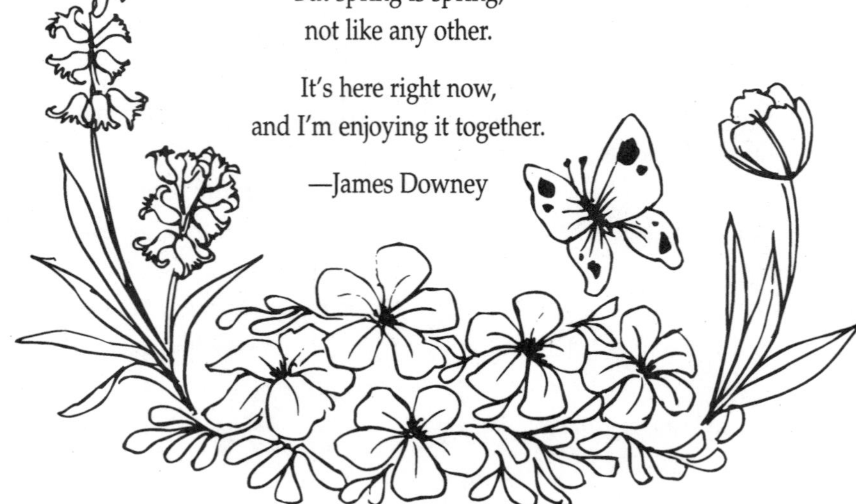

Name ______________________________ Date______________

Under each of the four seasons, brainstorm a list of thoughts, feelings, or images. Then on page 144, write your own seasonal poem.

The Four Seasons—My Brainstorming List

Summer

Fall

Winter

Spring

Name ______________________ Date ____________

A Super Seasonal Poem

____
Title

Name ______________________________ Date______________

HAIKU

Haiku are Japanese poems which have three lines and 17 syllables. They are about nature or the four seasons. Traditionally, the pattern for haikus is line one—5 syllables, line two—7 syllables, and line three—5 syllables. These poems have neither rhyme nor rhythm. They are created to evoke images of the natural world and our relationship to it. Six student samples appear below. After reading the poems, see if you can write your own haiku poems.

Haikus

Trees shedding crisp leaves
Cold winds blow them away
Piles of bright red, fire
—Carrie Matthews

Dark clouds loom above
Armies of wet droplets
Attack people passing by
—Jill Chang

Spring is finally here
New life comes to the world
Babies giggle with glee
—Emily Newman

Animals scavenging
Trees, desert bare
Grass dormant under snow
—Tyler Lamkey

Cold biting wind
Needles against my face
Winter's back
—Kiersten Nicholson

Trees bearing no leaves
Smoke swirling out of chimneys
Animals vanish
—Tiffany Stude

Name ______________________________ Date__________

Personal Narratives

Personal narratives are pieces of writing based on your own experiences. Any occasion can be the focus of a personal narrative. You might like to write about a special relative, holiday, birthday, baseball game, etc. The main characteristic of personal narratives is that they should be a focused piece of writing that describes a specific event in a clear and sharp manner. Personal narratives are often written in the first person. Their goal is to leave readers entertained or inspired, with a smile on their faces or tears in their eyes.

Below and on pages 147–161 are some examples of student-written personal narratives. Read and enjoy them. When you finish reading them, try writing a personal narrative of your own. You might begin by making a list of significant events in your life. Then brainstorm words or phrases associated with those events. In this way, your list could become the start of a story.

A Grandma Angel

"Maggie. Maggie. Honey, wake up." I could tell something was wrong. It was only 5:30 A.M. and my parents were sitting on the side of my bed. My mom's voice quivered as she spoke.

"What?" I asked half awake, knowing that what they were going to say, I wasn't going to like.

"Hi, Mags."

"Hi, Dad." I responded to my nickname. I was up now and could tell for sure something was going on by the expression on my dad's face. His eyes started to water so my mom took over.

"Honey, Grandma passed away earlier this morning. Dad is leaving to go to Oklahoma to be with his family, so give him a kiss good-bye."

I felt like a truck had just hit me. As soon as I heard "passed away," I burst out crying. I gave my father a kiss and he left to go to my sisters' Emily and Brianne's rooms to say good-bye to them. I cried myself back to sleep. I had another hour before I would have to wake up and get ready for school.

My alarm went off. My fingers stumbled around my night stand trying to find my alarm clock and turn the loud, obnoxious music off. I went down the winding stairs and into the kitchen. There I met mom sitting at the table alone drinking a cup of coffee. We exchanged greetings while I got myself something for breakfast. I sat down next to her and asked her some details about Grandma's death, trying to hold back the tears. I found out that she had died unexpectedly early in the morning and that my father's sister, Aunt Kelly, called to tell us what happened. I asked if I were to go to school. My mom said yes and I was to tell my teachers that I wouldn't be in school for the next two days due to my grandma's death. I also had to get all the homework I would miss. All of my teachers said, "Oh, I'm sorry." It made me feel uncomfortable. I didn't know what to say.

Name ______________________________ Date______________

My mom woke my sisters and me up early the next morning to catch a flight to Oklahoma. When we got to Oklahoma, my dad picked us up from the airport and we drove directly to my Aunt Kelly's house. We stayed at her house while we were in Oklahoma. The day we arrived in Oklahoma was also the day of my grandma's wake. There were two sessions. The first was around noon, and the second was around 7:00 P.M.

On the ride to the wake, everyone in the car was quiet. Everyone was in his or her own thoughts. All of my relatives and I walked into the building where the wake was being held. The man in charge of the funeral home showed us the room where Grandma was being waked. We walked into the room. It was filled with flowers. In the center of the room was my grandma lying peacefully in a coffin. I saw my grandmother lying still, and this is when I first realized that Grandma was really dead.

Whenever I remember my grandma's death, I remember myself sitting on a couch thinking, it can't be true, but knowing deep down inside her death really happened. A year later, I hold my grandma's beads that she wore. She was so beautiful and so funny. I wish I could just see her one more time and tell her how much I love her.

—Meredith McTernan

Name ______________________________ Date______________

My First Birthday

It was a hot summer day in the middle of June. June 18, 1984 to be exact. I was celebrating my first birthday in the living room of my house. My parents were waiting for one of their friends, Lucy, to arrive. At about 5:00 P.M., we ate dinner.

My grandpa called us, and my mom put me on the phone. I couldn't talk at the time, so I just listened to his voice. Two neighbors of ours, twins named Amy and Alex, came over to my party. The twins were two years old, and I had fun playing with them.

After dinner, we had my birthday cake. It was a German Black Forest cake with vanilla frosting and lots of chocolate sprinkles. It was surrounded by a ring of cherries. On the cake were three clown heads and one Winnie the Pooh candle. After everyone finished a piece of cake and a scoop of ice cream, it was time for me to open my presents.

My first gift was a blue Smurf walker. I could walk quite well at the time. However, sometimes, I was a little unsteady on my feet. Next, I got a white and yellow Playmates sandbox. I also got some clothes, stuffed animals, and plastic trucks. Amy and Alex gave me a stuffed elephant and a talking toy which named animals when I pulled on the cord on the side of it. My parents were careful not to give me toys to chew on because I had two upper and four lower teeth, and I always chewed on whatever I could find along my path.

I think that the presents I got that day helped me to learn to talk and to walk faster and better than I would have without them. The walker supported me until I could walk free of it and the pull-cord toy taught me to repeat the names of many animals. To this day, my parents have kept these presents, and I am sure they have because living to your first birthday is always a reason to celebrate.

—Les Swiecki

Name ______________________________ Date______________

Best Birthday

On July 11, 1996, I had the best birthday ever. I went to a Pearl Jam concert. Little did I know it would be a day I would never forget. My friends Collin and J. P. and my dad and I went to the event. Luckily, we went to the concert in Milwaukee, Wisconsin because two Pearl Jam concerts in Chicago had been canceled. The concert was held at the mammoth Marcus Amphitheater on the Summerfest grounds. Although our seats were in the midsection of Row A, Section 10, they were terrific. The only reason I could see above the heads of the crowd in front of me was because there was a walkway in front of us and no one could sit in it.

Before the show started, we ate dinner and bought souvenirs. I got a T-shirt with Mr. Point on it. The picture was abstract and surrounded by words all related to points. I thought the shirt was awesome.

The concert started with a band called The Frogs. They were terrible. The lead singer had on a green patent leather suit. The Frogs were nearly booed off the stage. Then a man with a microphone came on stage. He had blonde hair and was wearing a white tuxedo. Through my binoculars, the man's face looked like the face of Eddie Vedder, Pearl Jam's head singer. I asked myself, "How could this be?" I knew that Eddie Vedder had long, straight hair. But within seconds, the man on stage ripped off his wig and started to sing Pearl Jam's song, "Even Flow." I was shocked, it was Eddie Vedder. That was the coolest entrance I had ever seen. After a minute, the crowd was so loud I couldn't hear Eddie sing. The crowd went berserk. The noise continued for about four hours.

After the show, we drove home from Milwaukee to Barrington. This birthday night had been super. I had heard my favorite band, had gotten awesome souvenirs, had had dinner with two buddies, and went to a concert with my best friend, my dad.

—Tim Lardner

Name ______________________ Date ______________

Christmas Vacation

The day I've been waiting for has finally come. I'll get out of school and then the fun begins. No more waking up at 6:00 A.M. and having to go to school. Nope! Not that! I get to sleep in every day, until I want to wake up. The days will pass by quickly, waiting for that special day to come, Christmas. I love that day. I think it is the best holiday because of all the gifts, the family reunions, and of course, the wonderful food which is always so great. I can stuff myself to the limit. No more waiting in classrooms, waiting for the bell to ring so I can get my lunch and eat. Nope. I can eat whatever I want, whenever I want it. Not only do my vacation days consists of eating, they also consist of watching television. Since it is my vacation, I ask myself, "Why not just sit in front of the TV?" Eventually, I tear myself away from TV and go out in the snow to play with my friends. This makes the days pass and Christmas gets closer and closer.

The next thing I know, it is Christmas Eve. Annually on Christmas Eve, my family goes to our friends' house in Rockford. There we have dinner. We also have fun visiting with their daughters who are my brother's and my age. After eating, we put on a traditional nativity scene. We use stuffed animals and costumes to create the right atmosphere. After our performance, we drive back home. We head off to bed and dream about Christmas morning.

Soon, I wake up and rub my eyes. I look at the clock near my bed and see that it is 8:00. I jump out of bed and prance around my room filled with anticipation of what the day will bring. I'm not supposed to wake up my brother or parents because it's too early, and they are still sleeping. It just kills me to have to wait until they get up, when all I can think about are the presents under the tree with my name on them. Finally, when I can't wait any longer I go and wake up my brother. He finally gives in and gets up. Then we walk into my parents' room and wake them up. They tell us to get on our slippers and robes and meet them downstairs.

At last, we head into the kitchen for some breakfast. The aroma of coffee mingles with that of frying bacon and eggs. After breakfast, we get showers, change into our Christmas clothes and wait again. This time, we are waiting because my mom has to go to Arlington Heights to pick up my grandma. Finally, the two arrive, and we are given our stockings to open. I'm usually the first finished opening the little presents in my stocking, and then I must sit and wait while the others open theirs. Once again, I wait for what awaits me under the tree in the living room.

Name ______________________________ Date__________________

After what seems like a long, long time, we all go to the living room. First my brother and I exchange presents, then my parents, and then my grandmother. One by one, we open the boxes and bags. Then we exchange hugs and kisses and thank yous, and my brother and I play with some of our games.

Soon it's time to leave to go to my grandma's retirement home for brunch. This takes about 20 minutes. The meal consists of appetizers, baked ham, honey roasted turkey, and mashed potatoes. I fill my plate and enjoy the meal. After brunch, we drive home, and I sit on the couch and watch TV for awhile. Finally, we eat our Christmas dinner which is usually a big bowl of soup. After a little more TV, I get into my pajamas and get into bed.

The day after Christmas, my family usually goes on vacation. We pack our bags and take off for a few days. Some places we have been to lately are Cancun, Wisconsin, Florida, and on a Caribbean cruise. We come home rested and ready for what lies ahead.

At last, I get caught up on my homework and pack my backpack in preparation for the next day. I savor my Christmas vacation as it is a time to relax, time to be with friends, and best of all—time to be with my family who means so much to me. The night before school begins, I hop in bed and recall my vacation days and already think that I can't wait until next year.

—James Downey

Name ______________________________ Date__________

The Tennis Ball Man

I first noticed Gary about four summers ago. He stood about 5 feet 5 and had shaggy brown hair. He had a childish smile and if you looked into his eyes long enough, you would not see a man, but a lost child playing his own game in his own world.

The day he appeared was just another hot July day. The neighborhood kids were playing in their sprinklers and some were having balloon fights. When he came, he just walked around our neighborhood over and over again while bouncing three green tennis balls. He would not just bounce them, but he did amazing tricks with them. He could juggle them with one hand or bounce and throw them at the same time and catch them in one hand. And if that wasn't difficult enough, he could do this while skipping or running. Of course, it kind of scared us and our parents to see a man walking around and around our neighborhood throwing tennis balls into the air. They told us not to go near or talk to him, and even they kept their distance. But that did not stop us from watching him in awe and wonderment as he did all those tricks.

Now even though Gary's first day appearance clearly stands out in my mind, the next summer he came is the one I will always remember. I was standing in the safety of my yard watching him do his acrobaticlike tricks by the side of the lake. I didn't realize that he noticed me staring at him, but he did. And when he did, he started walking over towards me. I became a little frightened, but when I saw Gary smile, my worries just faded away. He gestured for me to hold the three tennis balls, and I did. Then he pretended to juggle them, and with no tennis balls in his hands, he made the trick look easy. Then I asked Gary in a simple way, "How?" He replied, "Soft hands," in a distorted sort of way. I then tried to mimic his movements and threw the balls into the air. I expected them to fall into place and be able to juggle quite easily. But the balls all fell to the ground and landed near my bare feet. I was disappointed. But then Gary smiled his childish smile and said, "That's okay, try again soon." I nodded and gave him back his three tennis balls. As he turned to walk away, I called out, "What's your name?" He gave me an unsure look, and I realized I had talked too fast for him to understand. I asked again, "What's your name?" at a slower speed and followed this with, "My name is Michelle." He smiled and said, "Me, Gary. You are Michelle." Then he turned and walked away, juggling those balls as he always had.

As the summers came and went, so did Gary. But we could always anticipate seeing him the next summer. Our parents became quite used to him being around and even though we knew his name was Gary, we decided a nickname would be more official, so we began to call him The Tennis Ball Man.

—Michelle Wheelhouse

Name ______________________________ Date______________

HERO STORIES

Friends and family make the perfect topics for pieces of writing. We often think of these people as **heroes** or extraordinary people. They have a great impact on our lives. Below and on pages 154–155 are some stories students have written about their heroes. Pete's hero is Mario Lemieux, the famous Canadian hockey player. Omar and Whitney selected their grandfathers as the focus of their pieces. Who is your hero? Write a story about him or her on pages 156–157.

My Hero

Mario Lemieux is my hero. He was born October 5, 1965, in Montreal, Quebec, Canada. He is 6' 4" and weighs 210 pounds. His name Lemieux means "the best" in French. He plays for the Pittsburgh Penguins hockey team in the NHL. In 1984, he was the Penguins' first pick. Mario became my hero because he is an outstanding player and a good role model. He is a good role model because he works extremely hard to accomplish what he sets out to do.

To play hockey, that is what Lemieux set out to do. Hockey has always been a big part of Mario's life. When he was ten years old, he and his brother locked their baby-sitter in the bathroom because she wanted to watch a movie instead of a hockey game on TV. Mario has sacrificed a lot for hockey. He became a pro hockey player when he was 18. Lemieux never finished high school. Mario is married to Nathalie, and they have a daughter named Lauren. Lemieux hates getting mobbed by fans, so he rarely goes out in public. In fact, he hasn't been to a movie theater in ten years.

In 1993, doctors discovered that Lemieux had Hodgkin's disease, a form of cancer. He had surgery and radiation treatments. Mario missed 62 games in the 1993–94 season because of back problems. Then in 1996, in a game against the New York Islanders, Mario scored his 500th NHL goal. Lemieux wears a special back pad to help his back when he is on the ice. Mario Lemieux will always remind me that I can do what I want if I put my mind to it. He also taught me that bad things can happen to good people.

—Pete Nimmer

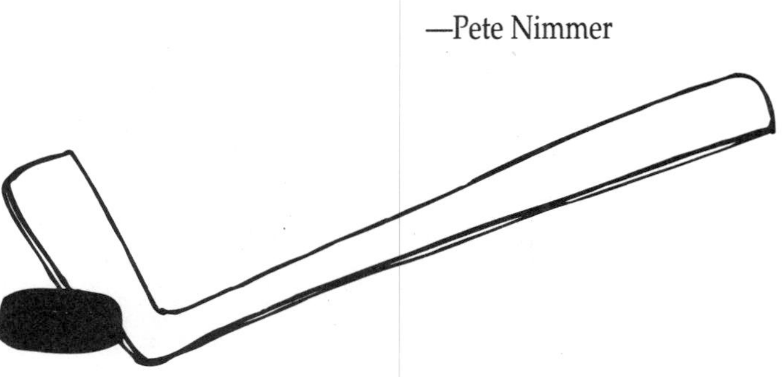

Name ______________________________ Date______________

My Hero

My grandfather, Wayne Siegworth is my hero. He was born in Burlington, Iowa on April 8, 1922, which happens to be the same day of the year I was born. He grew up the son of a school principal/farmer and homemaker. He was the oldest of four sons and was looked up to by his brothers.

Grandpa Siegworth's family moved to central Illinois. After graduating from high school, he entered the Air Force to serve our country in World War II. He was stationed in the Philippines Islands. He flew a bomber plane called an A20. He flew many successful missions during the war.

After World War II, my grandfather attended Illinois State University. During his years there, he met and married my grandmother, Betty. From ISU, he continued his college education at the University of Illinois. After teaching there for a few years, came the births of their son, my father, Robert Wayne, and their daughter, and my aunt, Sandra Kay.

Later, the Siegworth family moved to Barrington. For the next 32 years, my grandfather taught chemistry and coached sports at Barrington High School. Since retiring in 1984, my grandparents have remained active and have traveled a lot. Although I only get to see my grandfather about six months a year, I really enjoy being with him. Every time I see him, I look at him and think of all the wonderful things he has done with his life.

—Whitney Siegworth

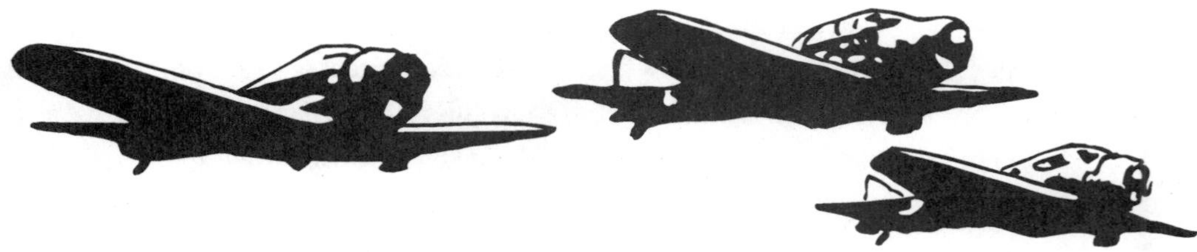

Name ______________________________ Date______________

My Hero

My hero would probably be my grandpa. I think my grandpa is a hero because he proved himself to be a hero with all of the medals he received from doing his job as a police commissioner. My grandfather was greatly respected by the people of India because of his good deeds. Since he died when I was two, I only know about my grandfather from stories my parents and relatives have told me.

My grandfather was a police commissioner. Whenever robbers or serious law breakers committed crimes, he would take over the investigation. My father told me that my grandfather was very brave and was very determined. He treated people the way he wanted to be treated. My grandfather was very kind.

Grandfather was awarded five medals for his work with the Indian police department. He received more medals that most other police commissioners. Some medals are for gallantry, others are the president's award. Grandfather got one of his gallantry medals when he caught a group of 45 thieves. It was very hard to catch the thieves because they would steal money and food from the richest people in the village and then donate food and money to the people of the village and keep some for themselves. My grandfather followed the thieves from village to village, but the people of the village would not help my grandfather catch the thieves. Finally, my grandfather surrounded one village with the help of two-hundred troops on horseback. At four o'clock in the morning, they surprised the thieves and captured them.

I think my grandfather is a hero because of his courage, bravery, and determination. My father says that even today, elder officers in the Indian police force remember my grandfather and speak about his good deeds. Even though my grandfather and his family were not rich, he was famous. Because of all the good things my grandfather did, he is my hero.

—Omar Shaikh

Name ______________________________ Date__________

Who's Your Hero?

Now that you have finished reading the hero stories by several students, make a list of relatives or friends you would consider to be your heroes. Then select one of these people to be the focus of your own hero story. Write your hero story below and on page 157. If you need more paper to finish your story, use notebook paper.

My Heroes

1. ______________ 6. ______________

2. ______________ 7. ______________

3. ______________ 8. ______________

4. ______________ 9. ______________

5. ______________ 10. ______________

My Hero Story

____

Title

Name ______________________________ Date______________

Name ______________________________ Date______________

SHORT STORIES

Short stories are fun to write. They are works of fiction that focus on a main character who faces a single problem. Below and on page 159 is a compelling story Courtney wrote of friendship. The characters in her story seem so real that is is hard to imagine that these are fictional characters. Read and see how this writer makes you think that her story could have really happened.

A Friend Till the End

My story is about Casey. Casey was my best friend and always will be. Casey wasn't popular. She had a scraggy brown mop of hair, buck teeth, and freckles. She had beautiful sky blue eyes that sparkled with excitement, but none of this made her attractive at all. Casey was teased a lot, but she never let it get her down.

She and I secretly made plans to run away. Tonight was the night. We agreed to meet at the park under the rotting, old birch tree near the baseball bleachers.

I was the first to arrive. It was freaky being in the park alone. Animals were making noises in the dead of night, or I wondered could it be a predator or an unknown man?

Then I noticed red-ruby eyes were watching me closely from a half eaten bush. My imagination, as usual, ran wild painting a picture in my mind of some lurking evil beast. Then I saw Casey coming. She was whistling an eerie tune.

Casey and I started walking out of the park. Neither of us knew exactly where we were going, but neither of us wanted to go back home where we weren't very happy. Finally, Casey said, "Maybe we should follow the train tracks." I thought that was a good idea and said, "Okay. After all, not many trains travel the tracks in the dead of night."

We walked in silence for quite some time. I was getting scared, and I knew Casey was too. Maybe we shouldn't have planned to run away, maybe we should just sneak back home. I wanted to tell these things to Casey. I wanted to say, "This is a stupid idea," but the words just wouldn't come out. I tried to tell Casey, but I was afraid that she would get mad at me if I told her what I was thinking.

"How far have we walked?" I called out. "How long have we been walking?" I continued. Now we had reached the bridge, and I could hear water running below. I heard it crashing on the jagged rocks I had seen before in the river's path.

Just as I began to relax a little, I felt the bridge begin to shake and shake. Soon it seemed as if the motion would toss us off the bridge. Casey screamed, "A ladder! Hurry! Come quick!" A train was heading our way. Its engine roared like an angry bear, and I was frozen in place. My hands and legs were like lead weights Superglued to the cold steel bar on the top of the ladder.

Name ____ Date________________

Casey was closer to the ladder, but she pushed me down first. She was screaming, "Hurry! Hurry!" The train's light bore down on us. I tried hard to get down as far as I could. The train was now blasting down the tracks at top speed. Casey, nearer to the train, put out her hand to me. I tried to catch it. The train just whizzed by. I heard Casey screaming as she fell from the bridge's ladder and plummeted into the river below. I reached her after a few minutes. Her head was bleeding from the cut she received when she fell onto the rocks in the river. All at once, my body began to shiver, and I began to sob. I knew Casey was dead, I also knew she risked her life for me by insisting that I go down the ladder first.

I have never felt so much guilt, so much grief, so much pain. If only we had asked someone for help, this would never have happened and my best friend, Casey, would still be alive.

—Courtney Boho

Name ______________________________ Date__________

A Super Short Story

Now it's your turn to think of a person, place, or event that you feel strongly about and that could become the focus of a short story. After you complete the people, places, and events relating to your story, begin writing your short story at the bottom of this page and finish it on page 161. If you need more paper to finish your story, use notebook paper.

People	Places	Events

My Short Story

____

Title

Name ______________________________ Date__________

Name ______________________________ Date__________

Expository Writing

Expository writing is one of the most common kinds of writing teachers ask their students to do. It is formal writing and is often thought of as report writing. It is nonfiction writing which presents facts or directions, or it explains ideas or defines terms. You may think of expository writing as the writing you do when your science or social studies teacher asks you to write a report.

Expository writing often requires you to do research to take notes, make an outline, and keep a list of the sources you use to write your paper. Several students wrote expository pieces comparing the terrestrial planets and the gas giant planets for both their science and English teachers. While each of these students had the same assignment, notice how unique each manuscript is. Use these essays as models when you are assigned to write a research report.

The Planets

The terrestrial planets and the gas giants have many similarities and differences. The names of the terrestrial planets are Earth, Mars, Mercury, and Venus. The names of the gas giants are Neptune, Saturn, Uranus, and Jupiter. Pluto isn't considered a gas giant or a terrestrial planet because it doesn't share their same characteristics. The other eight planets have many similarities and differences.

A first similarity about both planet groups is they revolve around the sun in an elliptical orbit. Another similarity is both are spherical. The body they revolve around is the same. They both revolve around the sun. These are just some of the similarities that these two types of planets have in common. They also have some of the differences.

For example, size of the planets is very different. The gas giants are big, while the terrestrial planets are small. Location is another difference. The gas giants are farther away from the sun than the terrestrial planets. The number of moons is a further difference, the terrestrial planets have zero to two moons, while the gas giants have eight to nineteen moons. The composition is another difference. These are just a few differences. There are some more.

The rings on each of the types of planets are different. The gas giants have rings while the terrestrial planets don't have any rings. The surface of the planets is different. The gas giants' surface is gas and the terrestrial planets' surface is made of rock and metal.

The planets have several similarities and differences between them. All of the similarities are they both revolve around the sun, and they have a spherical shape. Size, location, surface, rings, and moons are differences between the two types of planets. The subject of the solar system is very interesting and there are still many things yet to be discovered about the planets.

—Jeff Pope

Name ______________________________ Date______________

The Terrestrial Planets and The Gas Giants

There are two types of planets in our solar system. The name given to one type is the Terrestrial Planets. The Terrestrial Planets are Mercury, Venus, Earth, and Mars. The second type of planets are the Gas Giants. The Gas Giants are Jupiter, Saturn, Uranus, and Neptune. These two kinds of planets have many similarities and differences which include their position in the solar system, cores, and the surfaces.

These planets are closer to the sun, have metal cores, and have a hard rock or water surface. The names of the Terrestrial Planets are Mercury, Venus, Earth, Mars, and Pluto. The second group of planets are the Gas Giants. These planets are large, have a fast rotation speed, and have a gas surface. The names of the Gas Giants are Jupiter, Saturn, Uranus, and Neptune. There are many similarities and differences between the Terrestrial Planets and Gas Giants.

The Terrestrial Planets and Gas Giants both revolve around the sun. Both groups have similar elliptical orbits around the sun. The Gas Giants and Terrestrial Planets all receive light and energy from the sun. Everyday the sun gives off light and energy to all of the nine planets. Both groups of planets have center cores. All the planets have a spherical core in the direct center of the planet. These are ways in which all the Terrestrial Planets and the Gas Giants are similar.

One difference between the Terrestrial Planets and the Gas Giants is the size. The Gas Giants are greatly larger than the Terrestrial Planets. The location of the planets in the solar system is also very different. The Terrestrial Planets are closer to the sun than the Gas Giants with the exception of Pluto. The surface of the planets has a small variety too. The Terrestrial Planets all have a hard rock or water surface; while the Gas Giants have surfaces consisting of gasses. Those are ways in which the Terrestrial Planets and the Gas Giants are different.

The core of the planets also has a vast difference of composition. The Terrestrial Planets have a metal core; while the Gas Giants have a small hydrogen core. There is also a difference in the planets' rotation speed. The Gas Giants rotate much faster than the Terrestrial Planets. Another difference are the ring systems found around the Gas Giants. Only the Gas Giants have ring systems which can consist of thousands of rings. Those are many differences between the Terrestrial Planets and the Gas Giants.

This paper has stated and described the similarities and differences between the Terrestrial Planets and Gas Giants. The similarities between the Terrestrial Planets and the Gas Giants are the revolutions' of the planets, both have cores, and all planets receive light and energy from the sun. Differences between the Terrestrial Planets and the Gas Giants are the size, location, surface, cores, rotation speeds, and the ring systems. Based on the previous information, people can educate themselves on our planets' similarities and differences. This information could be useful to many people such as geologists, astronomers, botanists, and many other people.

—Christy Anton

CHAPTER 21
WRITING IDEAS

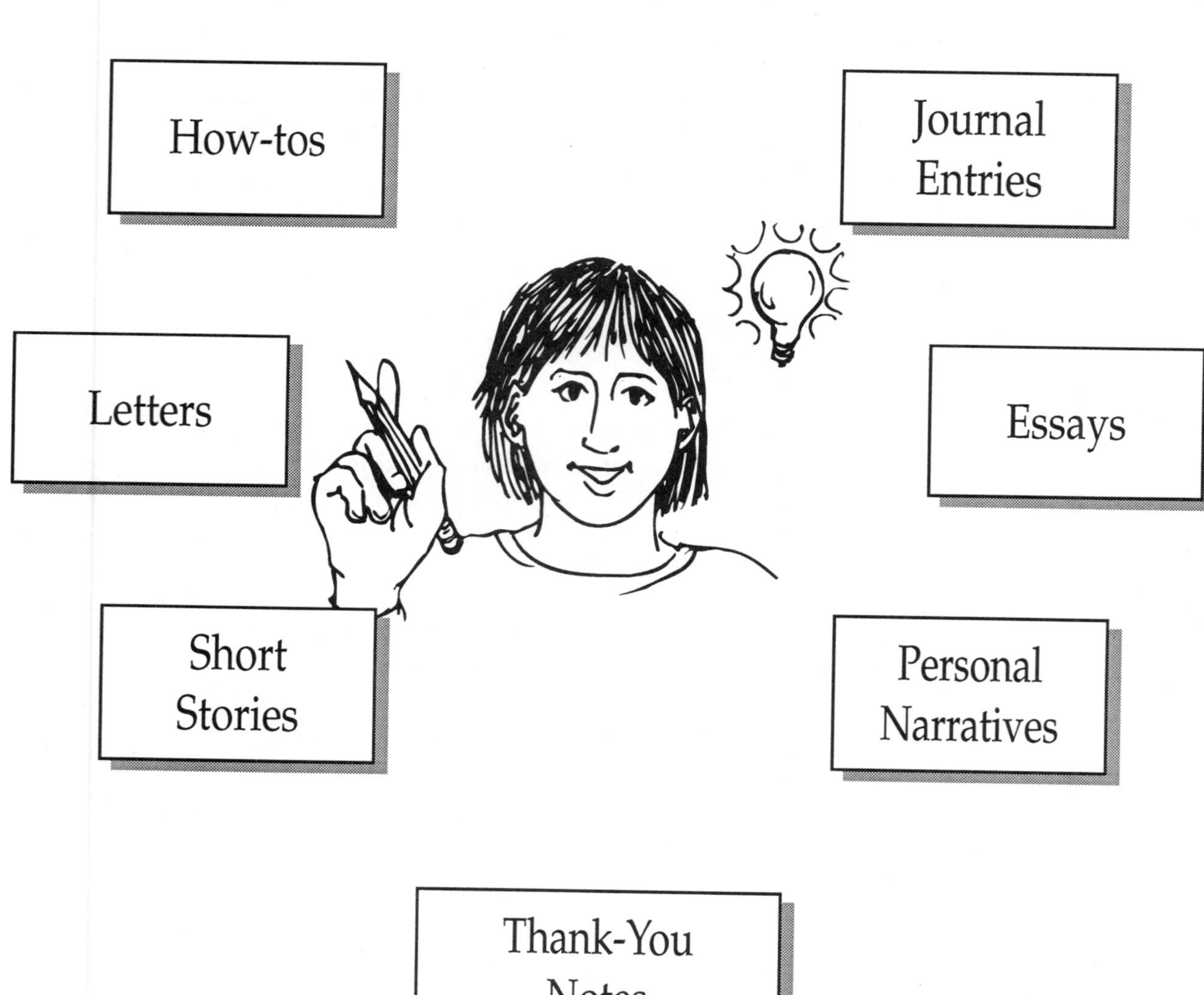

WRITING IDEAS

"'Where do writers get their ideas?' people often ask me.
'Where do they get their ideas?' they want to know.
It sounds as if there might be a secret place, one only
writers know about, where ideas roam wild like horses.
All we writers have to do is round them up, lasso one, and lead it home."

—Sandy Asher

If you are stuck for a writing idea, and you can't seem to fill the blank page on your desk, use the list of topics below and on pages 166–170 to stimulate you to write. Remember, you have a lot to write about because you have had a lot of life experiences. Sometimes it just takes the right prompt to get you started. You can use this list of over 100 prompts to compose poems, stories, essays, persuasive pieces, letters, personal narratives, descriptive paragraphs, how-tos, letters, journal entries, thank-you notes, etc.

1. Who am I?
2. My pet peeve is . . .
3. My first pet . . .
4. The first time I met __________, I just knew we'd be friends.
5. The birthday I'll never forget
6. The best book I've ever read
7. My favorite book character
8. If I could run the school for one day, I'd . . .
9. My favorite teacher
10. The most memorable vacation I had with my family
11. My favorite song
12. The easiest class for me

Name ____ Date________________

13. My best year in school
14. My favorite toy
15. My most interesting relative
16. __________ is my sports hero because . . .
17. A meal I will never forget
18. One boring afternoon, my friend and I . . .
19. My best friend in my neighborhood
20. I always . . .
21. I really dislike . . .
22. When I was five, I . . .
23. The one thing about me that nobody knows is . . .
24. When my best friend dropped me, I . . .
25. I really got in trouble with my family when . . .
26. I'm a whiz in the kitchen at . . .
27. If I could change one thing about me, it would be . . .
28. A Very Special Christmas (Hanukkah)
29. Flowers make me . . .
30. The happiest day of my life was . . .
31. The saddest day of my life was . . .
32. I'll never forget when . . .
33. My hero is . . .
34. I collect . . .
35. My first bike
36. The sport I excel in is . . .
37. I love to cook . . .
38. The dream that frightened me most was . . .
39. I will always keep my __________ because . . .
40. I hate wearing __________ because . . .

Name ______________________________ Date______________

41. Kids teased me when . . .
42. Being the new kid at school is . . .
43. In my family, I'm the best at . . .
44. Last summer, I . . .
45. My funniest experience is . . .
46. At our family reunion, I . . .
47. Our house is . . .
48. School is . . .
49. My first house
50. My first job
51. My next-door neighbors . . .
52. The most unusual person in my neighborhood is . . .
53. On my block, I see . . .
54. I got in trouble with my in-line skates when . . .
55. I once saw . . .
56. I remember the time when I had to do the laundry and . . .
57. I remember the time I had to cook dinner and . . .
58. I'll never forget my trip to the emergency room when . . .
59. If I could, I'd live in . . .
60. After I told my mom (my dad) the bad news, . . .
61. My grandmother is . . .
62. My grandfather is . . .
63. My aunt is . . .
64. My uncle is . . .
65. I'll never forget when . . .
66. If I lived on a far and distant planet, I . . .
67. The hardest day at school for me was . . .
68. At the concert, . . .

Name ______________________________ Date______________

69. My brother . . .
70. Everyone laughed when . . .
71. The satellite was shining brilliantly when . . .
72. I was upset by the news that . . .
73. My sister . . .
74. I was upset when . . .
75. I felt stupid the day I . . .
76. When I first woke, I heard . . .

Questions to explore . . .

77. Why are some people lonely?
78. Why don't I have red hair?
79. Why is the sun brighter than any other star?
80. Why are some people arrogant?
81. What if we could live beneath the ocean?
82. What if I could live on Mars?
83. What if dinosaurs were still alive?
84. Why do some people insult others?

How did . . . stories

85. the dog get its tail?
86. the cat get its meow?
87. the black widow get its sting?
88. an armadillo get its armor?
89. the Great Dane become so tall and the Chihuahua become so small?
90. a Dalmatian get its spots?

Name ______________________________ Date______________

Some "About Me" themes

91. My invisible friend and I
92. My worst enemy
93. What would happen if . . .
94. The most important day of my life
95. My family
96. The best day of my life

How-to's . . .

97. Make tacos or any other kind of food
98. Select a friend
99. Cut the grass
100. Play chess

Places or things to write about . . .

101. My secret place
102. My bedroom
103. The river
104. Our garage
105. The school bus
106. The hallway at school
107. A place I wish I could visit
108. A far and distant land
109. In the land of make-believe

Other things to write about . . .

110. A family tale
111. Someone who wronged you

Name ______________________________ Date__________

112. Saying you are sorry for something that happened
113. Getting your anger out
114. The death of a pet
115. A time when you were lost
116. A time when you were sick
117. Your favorite color
118. Your most reckless moment
119. The worst decision you ever made
120. A time you lost your temper
121. Pretend you have been invited by NASA to join its team of astronauts.

How do you feel?

122. What is the first success you can remember?
123. List all the images that come to mind when you hear the word *midnight*.
124. If I could change the world, . . .
125. The first time I saw __________, I . . .
126. The best vacation I ever had was . . .

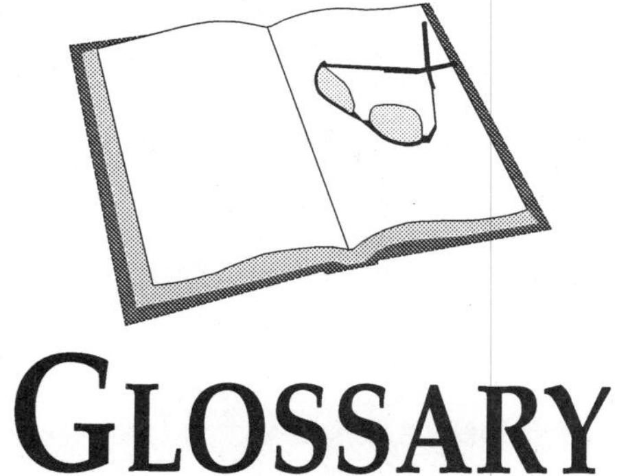

GLOSSARY

acrostic—formula poems in which the first line begins with the first letter of a word spelled vertically

anthology—a collection of student writings

audience—the person or people for whom a writer writes a piece of writing

brainstorming—a prewriting technique used to gather writing ideas. In appearance, it can be free form, a map, a cluster, a tree, a list, or another shape. This is sometimes referred to as a writer's map.

clustering—a brainstorming technique in which the writer groups words or phrases together based on a given topic or subject

conferencing—meeting with peers, a writing group, and/or a teacher to discuss and improve a piece of writing

drafts—a number of writings done by the writer using pen and paper or a word processor in the writing process. Usually, there will be a first and second draft before the final copy of a paper is done.

editing—a series of activities a writer engages in to improve and polish his or her manuscript. There are several kinds of editing techniques including self, peer, and adult.

expository—usually a 5-paragraph essay written to explain, compare or contrast, or analyze a topic

final copy—the last phase of the writing process when the manuscript is ready for publication and sharing

first draft—a writer's first attempt at writing a manuscript whether it be a poem, essay, or story. Time should be spent in writing the piece, not in stopping to edit it.

free verse—poetry which is not rhymed and does not have a required, specific number of lines

genre—a French word which means a classification or kind of writing. Genres include mystery, romance, science fiction, fantasy, sports, etc.

haiku—a type of Japanese poem which contains three lines with a 5, 7, 5 syllabic pattern. Themes include seasons and nature.

listing—a brainstorming technique in which the writer makes a list of ideas, thoughts, words, or phrases based on a first impression of a topic

manuscript—a piece of writing which may be a poem or play, report or rubric, narrative or note, even a letter or a list. This term is used throughout the book.

mapping—a prewriting technique used to generate ideas in preparation for a piece of writing

notebook—a spiral or binder in which writers keep their writings, lists, notes, ideas, clippings, etc.

peer editing—correcting of a manuscript by a person of the writer's age or interest group

personal narrative—writing based on the writer's experiences. Some parts may be fictionalized to fit the story. It should have a specific, limited focus.

portfolio—a place in which writings are stored. It includes writings from the draft stage to false starts as well as unfinished and finished manuscripts. A well-rounded portfolio will have a variety of writings (see manuscript), and it may include writings from several disciplines.

prewriting—a technique used to explore and gather writing ideas

proofreading—the stage in the writing process in which a writer carefully reads a draft to correct mistakes in content and style, as well as errors with grammar, usage, mechanics, paragraph placement, etc.

publishing—the last stage of the writing process when the writer makes a final, clean copy of a paper

purpose—the reason for writing. The writer writes to be creative, to entertain, to explain, to inform, to explore, or to persuade.

revision—techniques used to change and improve a manuscript. It includes proofreading, editing, conferencing, and various drafts of a paper.

sharing—when the writer shares his or her manuscript with his or her audience. Sharing can be public or private.

treeing—a brainstorming technique in which the writer branches ideas off the main stem of a topic, word, or thought

voice—writer's style which reveals his or her personality

web—a clustering technique used to help a writer find writing ideas

word processing—a program on a computer that enables writers to eliminate many boring or repetitive tasks involved in the writing process. It often includes spell check, thesaurus, dictionary, and word count components.

writing—the stage in which a writer puts his or her ideas into sentences and paragraphs and follows a plan for presenting those ideas

INDEX

BIBLIOGRAPHY

Aber, Linda Williams. *101 Ways to Boost Your Writing Skills.* NY: Troll Associates, 1996.

Amberg, Jay and Mark Larson. *The Creative Writing Handbook.* Glenview, IL: Scott, Foresman & Company, 1992.

Asher, Sandy. *Where Do You Get Your Ideas?* NY: Walker and Company, 1987.

Atchity, Kenneth. *A Writer's Time.* NY: W. W. Norton & Co., 1986.

Atwell, Nancie. *In the Middle: Writing, Reading, and Learning With Adolescents.* Portsmouth, NH: Heinemann: 1987.

Bauer, Marion Dane. *What's Your Story?* NY: Clarion Books, 1992.

Benjamin, Carol Lea. *Writing For Kids.* NY: Harper & Row, Publishers, 1985.

Block, Lawrence. *Writing the Novel From Plot to Print.* Cincinnati, OH: Writer's Digest Books, 1979.

Bradbury, Ray. *Zen in the Art of Writing.* NY: Bantam Books, 1990.

Buchman, Dian Dincin and Seli Groves. *The Writer's Digest Guide to Manuscript Formats.* Cincinnati, OH: Writer's Digest Books, 1987.

Burroway, Janet. *Writing Fiction.* Boston, MA: Little, Brown and Company, 1987.

Bushman, John H. and Kay Parks Bushman. *Using Young Adult Literature in the English Classroom.* NY: Macmillan Publishing Co., 1993.

Calkins, Lucy McCormick. *The Art of Teaching Writing.* Portsmouth, NH: Heinemann: 1986.

Carr, Robyn. *Practical Tips for Writing Popular Fiction.* Cincinnati, OH: Writer's Digest Books, 1992.

Carroll, David L. *A Manual of Writer's Tricks.* NY: Paragon House, 1990.

Charbonneau, Eileen. "If You Want to Write a Young Adult Novel . . .," *The Writer.* Boston, MA: April 1995.

Clark, Thomas, Bruce Woods, et al. *The Writer's Digest Guide to Good Writing.* Cincinnati, OH: Writer's Digest Books: 1994.

Edelstein, Scott. *30 Steps to Becoming a Writer and Getting Published.* Cincinnati, OH: Writer's Digest Books, 1993.

Elbow, Peter. *Writing With Power.* NY: Oxford University Press, 1981.

Elbow, Peter. *Writing Without Teachers.* NY: Oxford University Press, 1973.

Flesch, Rudolf and A. H. Lass. *A New Guide to Better Writing.* NY: Popular Library, 1963.

Flesch, Rudolf. *How to Write, Speak, and Think More Effectively.* NY: New American Library, 1960.

Goldberg, Natalie. *Long Quiet Highway.* NY: Bantam Books, 1993.

Goldberg, Natalie. *Wild Mind: Living the Writer's Life.* NY: Bantam Books, 1990.

Goldberg, Natalie. *Writing Down the Bones.* Boston, MA: Shambhala, 1986.

Grant, Janet E. *Young Person's Guide to Becoming a Writer.* White Hall, VA: Shoe Tree Press, 1986.

Graves, Donald H. *Writing: Teachers and Children at Work.* Portsmith, NH: Heinemann Educational Books, 1983.

Henderson, Kathy. *Market Guide for Young Writers 1986-87 Edition.* Sandusky, MI: Savage Publishing, 1986.

Lloyd, Pamela. *How Writers Write.* Melbourne, Australia: Thomas Nelson Australia, 1987.

Madden, David. *Revising Fiction: A Handbook for Writers.* NY: New American Library, 1988.

McCord, David. *One at a Time.* NY: Little, Brown, 1986.

Mueller, Lavonne and Jerry D. Reynolds. *Creative Writing.* Lincolnwood, IL: National Textbook Company, 1991.

Naylor, Phyllis Reynolds. *How I Came to Be a Writer.* NY. Aladdin Books, 1987.

Otfinoski, Steve. *Scholastic Guides: Putting It in Writing.* NY: Scholastic Inc., 1993.

Peck, Richard. *Love and Death at the Mall: Teaching and Writing for the Literate Young.* NY: Delacorte Press, 1994.

Provost, Gary. *Beyond Style: Mastering the Finer Points of Writing.* NY: New American Library, 1982.

Provost, Gary. *The Freelance Writer's Handbook.* Cincinnati, OH: Writer's Digest Books, 1982.

Provost, Gary. *Make Every Word Count.* Cincinnati, OH: Writer's Digest Books, 1986.

Provost, Gary. *100 Ways To Improve Your Writing.* NY: New American Library, 1985.

Rico, Gabriele Lusser. *Writing the Natural Way.* Los Angeles, CA: J.P. Tarcher, Inc., 1983.

Stanek, Lou Willett. *So You Want to Write A Novel.* NY: Avon Books, 1994.

Stanek, Lou Willett. *Thinking Like a Writer.* NY: Random House, 1994.

Tchudi, Susan and Stephen. *The Young Writer's Handbook.* NY: Aladdin Books, 1984.

Terban, Marvin. *Scholastic Guides: Checking Your Grammar.* NY: Scholastic Inc., 1993.

Vogler, Christopher. *The Writer's Journey: Mythic Structure for Storytellers and Screenwriters.* Studio City, CA: Michael Wiese Productions, 1992.

Yates, Elizabeth. *Someday You'll Write.* NY: E.P. Dutton & Co., 1962.

Zinsser, William. *On Writing Well.* NY: Harper & Row, Publishers, 1988.

Zinsser, William. *Writing to Learn.* NY: Harper & Row, Publishers, 1988.